400 Calorie Dinners

Satisfying, Guilt-Free, Real-Life Meals

Printed in the United States of America
by G&R Publishing Co.

Published By:

507 Industrial Street
Waverly, IA 50677

ISBN-13: 978-1-56383-316-8
ISBN-10: 1-56383-316-6
Item #7104

TABLE OF CONTENTS

THE DIETER'S DINNER

Congratulations!

By purchasing this book, you have taken an important step in managing a healthy lifestyle. Tracking the amount of calories you consume has proven to be a successful way to lose or maintain a healthy weight. Most dieting programs (low-fat, carb-free, limiting sugars, low-glycemic eating) all boil down to eating fewer calories than you burn.

In addition, many Americans underestimate the amount of calories they are consuming on a daily basis by almost 600! That's a lot of unknown calories that could potentially add up to extra pounds and unwanted fat.

This book is packed with meal-time recipes that will help you take the guesswork out of calorie counting. Each meal, including sides, is 400 calories or less. And each recipe comes complete with side dish suggestions and recipes, giving you hundreds of possibilities for a healthy, filling and delicious dinner. Since food portions, brands and packaging can vary, calories and fat content listed are an estimate. But rest assured: all these meals are very close to 400 calories or less, and often, they are quite a bit less!

What are calories?

A calorie is a unit of measurement, but it doesn't measure length or weight. A calorie is actually a unit of energy. For example, when you read a portion of food contains 100 calories, the measurement is describing how much energy you get from eating that particular portion of food.

Calories are very important – your body needs them for energy, but eating too many calories can lead to weight gain. This is why it's important to count calories when you are trying to lose or maintain your weight. If you take in more calories than you burn, you will gain weight. If you take in fewer calories than you burn, you will lose weight. If you balance the two, you will maintain your weight.

Calories should not be cut back so much that your energy needs are not met. The number of calories you need depends primarily on your age, gender and activity level. Consult a doctor or nutritionist to determine what your calorie intake should be.

The combination of counting calories and eating foods rich in nutrients is the best way to maintain your weight and live a healthy lifestyle.

THE DIETER'S DINNER

Determining calories in food

All food and beverages, except for water, contain calories. Even if a label says that a food contains 0 calories, that means the serving size of the food contains trace calories, or under 1 calorie per serving.

To determine the amount of calories in a certain food, scientists separate the noncaloric and caloric compounds of the food. The noncaloric compounds are things like the amount of water and minerals. The caloric compounds are divided into the fat, alcohol, protein and carbohydrates found within the food. Then, the weight of each caloric compound is mulitplied according to the chart below to determine the total amount of calories in the food.

Each gram of fat	9 calories
Each gram of alcohol	7 calories
Each gram of protein	4 calories
Each gram of carbohydrates	3.75 calories

Medium (7″) banana = approximately 110 calories

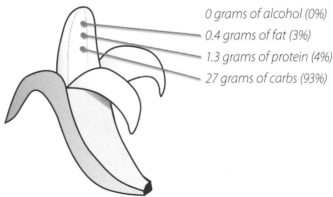

0 grams of alcohol (0%)
0.4 grams of fat (3%)
1.3 grams of protein (4%)
27 grams of carbs (93%)

In addition to calories, another important number to check on labels is the calories from fat. Calories from fat are more easily converted into body fat than calories from protein or carbs. While a medium-size banana contains only 3.6 (or 3%) of its calories from fat, 1 cup of regular shredded Cheddar cheese contains 337 calories from fat, or about 74%.

THE DIETER'S DINNER

Rounding it out

The human body needs and gathers calories from all four caloric compounds. However, there are healthy and not-so-healthy choices within each category.

Fat: Fat contains more than twice the number of calories than in protein and carbohydrates, and all food agencies recommend eating fats sparingly. The type of fat consumed is often irrelevant from a weight-loss standard, since all fat contains 9 calories per gram. However, from a health viewpoint, it is important to ingest most of your caloric fat from vegetable fats and oils rather than animal fats. One slight exception to the rule is omega-3 fatty acids. Oily fish, such as salmon or herring, are a good source of omega-3s, which have proven to assist weight control and maintain good health.

Alcohol: Alcohol is a fairly high-calorie item, with 7 calories in each gram. Therefore, it is best to avoid or reduce alcohol intake if you are following a calorie-controlled diet. In addition, alcohol can increase your appetite as well as the amount of calories you consume. A small to moderate intake of alcohol per day (1 beer, 1 small glass of wine, or 1½ ounces of spirits) can be good for your health, but a higher intake puts you at risk of coronary heart disease, liver disease and some cancers.

Protein: Protein is essential for good health and building muscles, however, it is best to limit your consumption of protein from animals (cheese and meat) and increase your consumption of protein from vegetables (beans, nuts, soybeans and lentils). Multiply your weight by .37 to find your recommended daily minimum of grams of protein to consume. However, remember that almost every food item contains some percentage of protein, which adds up quickly. Over-intake of protein is not recommended for individuals with kidney disease, as it can cause health problems.

Carbohydrates: When choosing which carbs to eat, it is recommended to follow the Glycemic Index. Pick carbohydrates with a low-glycemic index rating (fruit, vegetables, whole grains), which take longer to digest and help maintain stable blood glucose levels. High-glycemic index foods (refined sugary foods, bagels, white breads, potatoes) contain "empty" carb calories, which can upset blood glucose levels and trigger food cravings.

3

QUICK RESTAURANT GUIDE

Though some major restaurants are courteous enough to list their nutritional information on menu boards, pamphlets and websites, you can never be exactly sure how many calories you are consuming when dining out. Your best bet is to go for the "lighter fare" items and ask for sauces or dressings on the side. Listed here are just a few of the *healthier* options that won't do you in when eating at these major chain restaurants.

Burger King	Calories	Fat
Egg & Cheese Croissan'wich	300	17 g
Tendergrill Chicken Garden Salad with Light Italian Dressing	360	20 g
Whopper Jr. without cheese or mayo, with a side Garden Salad	365	12 g

Carl's Jr. and Hardee's	Calories	Fat
Charbroiled BBQ Chicken Sandwich	360	4.5 g
⅓ lb. Low Carb Thickburger	420	32 g

In-N-Out Burger	Calories	Fat
Hamburger with onion, tomato, lettuce and ketchup	310	10 g
Double-Double Hamburger Protein Style	350	22 g

McDonald's	Calories	Fat
Asian Salad with Grilled Chicken and Low-Fat Sesame Ginger Dressing	180	12.5 g
Egg McMuffin	300	12 g
6-piece Chicken McNuggets with 1 packet BBQ sauce	300	19 g
Quarter Pounder without cheese	410	7 g

Wendy's	Calories	Fat
Ultimate Chicken Grill Sandwich	320	7 g
Single Burger with everything	430	20 g
Small Chili and 5-piece Crispy Chicken Nuggets	450	21 g

QUICK RESTAURANT GUIDE

Arby's	Calories	Fat
Martha's Vineyard Salad with Light Buttermilk Ranch Dressing	389	14 g
Super Roast Beef	440	19 g
Chicken Cordon Bleu Sandwich	488	18 g

Chipotle	Calories	Fat
Chicken Burrito Bowl with lettuce, black beans, green tomatillo salsa and sour cream	489	22 g
Carnitas Salad with pinto beans, green tomatillo salsa and cheese	495	22 g
Crispy Steak Tacos with corn salsa, red tomatillo salsa and romaine lettuce	543	21 g

Taco Bell	Calories	Fat
2 Grilled Steak Soft Tacos, Fresco Style	320	9 g
2 Spicy Chicken Soft Tacos	340	12 g
Chicken Fiesta Taco Salad without the shell	470	24 g

Jimmy John's	Calories	Fat
Vegetarian Sub with alfalfa sprouts, tomatoes, onion, cucumber and avocado spread	290	1.5 g
Turkey Breast Slim Sub with alfalfa sprouts, tomatoes, onion, cucumber and avocado spread	426	2 g
Totally Tuna Sub	507	20 g

Quiznos	Calories	Fat
Small Honey Bourbon Chicken on Wheat Bread	310	4 g
Small Tuscan Turkey on Rosemary Parmesan Bread without cheese	390	14 g
Small Black Angus Sandwich	520	16.5 g

Subway	Calories	Fat
Oven Roasted Chicken Breast Salad with Fat-Free Italian Dressing	175	2.5 g
6-inch Double Roast Beef Sub	360	7 g
6-inch Steak & Cheese	400	12 g

QUICK RESTAURANT GUIDE

Domino's	Calories	Fat
2 slices 12" Crunchy Thin Crust Ham & Pineapple Pizza	300	16 g
2 slices 12" Crunchy Thin Crust Deluxe Feast	470	32 g

Papa John's	Calories	Fat
2 slices 12" Original Crust Spinach Alfredo Pizza	400	16 g
2 slices 12" Original Crust Garden Fresh Pizza	400	14 g
2 slices 14" Thin Crust Cheese Pizza	480	26 g

Pizza Hut	Calories	Fat
2 slices 12" Fit n' Delicious Pizza with green pepper, red onion and diced tomatoes	300	8 g
2 slices 12" Thin 'N Crispy Ham & Pineapple Pizza	360	12 g
2 slices 12" Thin 'N Crispy Pepperoni & Mushroom Pizza	380	16 g

Chick-fil-A	Calories	Fat
Chargrilled Chicken Sandwich	270	3.5 g
8-pack Chicken Nuggets with Barbecue Sauce	305	13 g
Southwest Chargrilled Salad with Fat-Free Honey Mustard Dressing	360	8 g

KFC	Calories	Fat
Honey BBQ KFC Snacker	210	3 g
Roasted BLT Salad with Fat-Free Ranch Dressing	235	6 g
3 Crispy Strips with green beans and 3" corn on the cob	470	22 g

Popeyes	Calories	Fat
2 Mild Chicken Strips	250	10 g
Spicy Chicken (breast, thigh, leg and wing) skinless with breading removed	290	8.5 g

Quick Restaurant Guide

Applebee's	Calories	Fat
Grilled Cajun Lime Tilapia with Black Bean & Corn Salsa	310	6 g
Teriyaki Steak & Shrimp Skewers	370	7 g

Chili's	Calories	Fat
Old Timer Burger on a whole wheat bun	420	27 g
Chicken Fajita Pita	450	17 g
Sizzle & Spice Firecracker Tilapia with sautéed mushrooms, onions, bell peppers and steamed broccoli	470	23 g

Olive Garden	Calories	Fat
Chicken Giardino	448	11 g
Linguine Alla Marinara with one breadstick	691	9.5 g
Shrimp Primavera	706	18 g

Outback Steakhouse	Calories	Fat
Victoria Fillet with steamed vegetables	639	45 g
Prime Minister's Prime Rib with fresh veggies and sweet potato	730	39 g

Red Lobster	Calories	Fat
1.25 lb. Maine Lobster with cocktail sauce and seasoned broccoli	288	3 g
Garlic Grilled Jumbo Shrimp and a baked potato with pico de gallo	329	5 g
Broiled Flounder and a garden salad with red wine vinaigrette	344	10 g

Ruby Tuesday	Calories	Fat
White Bean Chicken Chili with Tomato and Mozzarella Salad	370	15 g
7 oz. Top Sirloin with green beans and sautéed portabella mushrooms	464	24 g
Creole Catch with Couscous and green beans	580	26 g

SIMPLE SUBSTITUTIONS

Sometimes making a meal healthy is as simple and painless as swapping out certain ingredients for others.

If your recipe calls for:	Try using:
All-purpose flour	Whole-wheat flour for ½ of the all-purpose flour
Bacon	Canadian bacon, turkey bacon or lean prosciutto
Butter or margarine	Applesauce for ½ of the butter or margarine
Canned tuna in oil	Canned tuna in water
Chicken thigh with skin	Chicken breast without skin
Chopped nuts (1 cup)	½ cup toasted chopped nuts for full flavor
Creamed soups	Fat-free milk-based soups or mashed potato flakes
Cream cheese	Fat-free or low-fat cream cheese, Neufchatel or low-fat cottage cheese
Eggs	Fat-free liquid egg substitute
Ground beef	Extra-lean or lean ground beef, chicken or turkey
Heavy cream	Evaporated skim milk
Oil for sautéing	Nonstick cooking spray for sautéing
Mayonnaise	Light mayonnaise, light creamy salad dressing or fat-free plain yogurt
Potatoes	Butternut squash or mashed cauliflower
Soy sauce	Low-sodium soy sauce, sweet-and-sour sauce or hot mustard sauce
Syrup	Pureed fruit or low-calorie, sugar-free syrup
Whole milk	Reduced-fat or fat-free milk

Casseroles
& Pasta

Chicken &
Brown Rice Casserole

Makes 4 servings

1 (8 oz.) can no-salt-added stewed tomatoes, undrained
¾ C. instant brown rice
½ C. raisins
1 T. lemon juice
3 tsp. curry powder
1 chicken bouillon cube
½ tsp. ground cinnamon
¼ tsp. salt
2 cloves garlic, minced
1 bay leaf, optional
3 (4 to 4.5 oz.) boneless, skinless chicken breast halves,
    trimmed of fat and cut into 1" pieces

Preheat the oven to 350°. In a large skillet over medium-high heat, combine 1 cup water with the stewed tomatoes with liquid, brown rice, raisins, lemon juice, curry powder, bouillon cube, cinnamon, salt, garlic and bay leaf. Bring the mixture to a boil, then stir in the chicken pieces; boil for 3 minutes. Transfer the mixture to a 1-quart baking dish; cover and bake for 45 minutes, stirring once or twice, until the rice is tender and the chicken is cooked through.

Serving size: *¼ of casserole (about 1¼ cups)*
Calories: *243*
Fat: *2 g*

Suggested sides: *Lemony Green Beans (68 calories, page 100) or Tasty Breaded Brussels (75 calories, page 109).*

Baked Shells with Mushrooms & Cheese

Makes 4 servings

1 C. uncooked medium shell pasta
2 C. tomato sauce
1 C. diced fresh mushrooms
½ C. crumbled firm silken tofu
½ C. shredded part-skim mozzarella cheese
¼ C. grated Parmesan cheese

Preheat the oven to 400°. Cook pasta in a large pot of boiling, lightly salted water for 8 to 10 minutes, or until al dente; drain. In a medium bowl, combine tomato sauce, mushrooms and tofu; stir in cooked pasta. Combine mozzarella and Parmesan cheeses in a separate bowl. Spread half of the pasta mixture across the bottom of a 1-quart baking dish; top with half of the cheese. Repeat the layers. Bake the casserole for 30 minutes, or until the cheese is lightly browned.

Serving size: ¼ of casserole (about 1 cup)
Calories: 221
Fat: 5.5 g

Suggested sides: Spiced Grape Salad (70 calories, page 103) or Seasoned Green Beans & Cherry Tomatoes (122 calories, page 112).

Feel the Burn!

One of the quickest ways to burn calories is jumping rope. Just about 7 minutes will burn 100 calories.

Turkey Vegetable Casserole

Makes 6 servings

¼ C. grated Parmesan cheese

2 T. extra-virgin olive oil, divided

2 (1.5 oz.) dinner rolls, torn into pieces

1½ C. chopped onion

1 C. chopped celery

1 tsp. salt, divided

1 (8 oz.) pkg. sliced fresh mushrooms

2 C. low-sodium turkey or chicken broth, divided

⅔ C. 1% low-fat milk

⅓ C. flour

3 C. chopped cooked light and dark turkey meat

1 C. fresh or frozen peas, thawed

1½ T. chopped fresh thyme

½ tsp. pepper

Preheat the oven to 350°. In a food processor, combine Parmesan cheese, 1 tablespoon olive oil and bread chunks; pulse until coarse crumbs measure about 1½ cups. Set aside crumb mixture. Heat the remaining 1 tablespoon olive oil in a medium skillet or Dutch oven over medium heat. Add onion and celery to the skillet; sauté for 6 minutes, or until tender. Stir in ¼ teaspoon salt and the mushrooms; sauté for an additional 5 minutes, stirring often. Add ½ cup broth to skillet and mix lightly. In a small bowl, combine milk and flour; gradually stir into liquid in skillet. Slowly stir in remaining 1½ cups broth and ½ teaspoon salt; cook for about 8 minutes or until mixture thickens. Add remaining ¼ teaspoon salt, cooked turkey, peas, thyme and pepper; cook for an additional 2 minutes or until heated through. Spoon the turkey mixture into a 9 x 13" baking dish sprayed with non-stick cooking spray. Sprinkle crumb mixture over turkey mixture. Bake casserole for 25 minutes, or until the edges are bubbling.

Serving size: ⅙ *of casserole (about 1 cup)*
Calories: 303
Fat: 9.7 g

Suggested sides: Spiced Grape Salad (70 calories, page 103) or Dilled Carrots (72 calories, page 114).

Ham & Bean Casserole with Biscuits

1½ C. frozen baby lima beans, thawed

¾ C. seeded and diced green bell pepper

⅓ C. chopped onion

1¼ C. chopped extra-lean ham (about 6 oz.)

1 C. shredded reduced-fat sharp Cheddar cheese

1 tsp. Worcestershire sauce

1 (14.75 oz.) can no-salt-added cream-style corn

6 T. skim milk

2 T. chopped green onion

¾ C. low-fat biscuit baking mix

Preheat the oven to 400°. Bring 1½ cups water to a boil in a medium saucepan over medium-high heat. Stir in the lima beans, bell pepper and onion; cover and cook for 5 minutes, then drain. In a large bowl, combine cooked bean mixture, ham, cheese, Worcestershire sauce and corn; mix until well combined. Spoon the mixture into a 2-quart baking dish sprayed with non-stick cooking spray; cover and bake for 20 minutes. Meanwhile, in a separate bowl, combine milk and green onion; stir in the baking mix. Divide the batter into 6 portions and drop by the spoonful over the casserole mixture into 6 biscuits. Bake, uncovered, for an additional 20 minutes, or until the biscuits are golden.

Serving size: ⅙ *of casserole (about ¾ cup plus 1 biscuit)*
Calories: *317*
Fat: *6.2 g*

Suggested side: *Balsamic Mandarin Salad (74 calories, page 101).*

Lighter Shepherd's Pie

Makes 6 servings

7 medium potatoes, peeled and cubed

1 lb. lean ground beef

2 beef bouillon cubes

1 chicken bouillon cube

1 tsp. dried rosemary

½ tsp. salt

1 tsp. pepper

1 tsp. steak seasoning

1 T. dried minced onion flakes

1½ C. frozen mixed vegetables

Preheat the oven to 350°. Bring a large pot of lightly salted water to a boil. Add cubed potatoes to the pot and cook until tender, about 15 minutes. Drain the pot, let the potatoes cool slightly, then mash and set aside. Sauté the ground beef in a large skillet over medium-high heat. Drain grease from skillet and return browned meat to skillet over medium heat. Stir in 1 cup water and the beef and chicken bouillon cubes. Stir in the rosemary, salt, pepper, steak seasoning and onion flakes. Mix in the frozen vegetables. Heat, stirring occasionally, until most of the water has evaporated. Spoon the mixture into a 2-quart baking dish sprayed with non-stick cooking spray. Spread the mashed potatoes over the casserole. Bake the casserole for 20 to 30 minutes, or until the potatoes begin to brown.

Serving size: ⅙ of pie (about 2 cups)
Calories: 384
Fat: 10 g

Suggested side: ½ cup shredded steamed cabbage (16 calories) or ½ cup steamed sugar snap peas (13 calories).

Broccoli Noodle Toss

Makes 4 servings

⅔ lb. uncooked rigatoni noodles (about 11 oz.)
2 C. broccoli florets
¼ C. grated Parmesan cheese
4 tsp. extra-virgin olive oil
4 tsp. minced garlic
Pepper to taste

Cook pasta in a large pot of boiling, lightly salted water for 8 to 10 minutes, or until al dente; drain and set aside. Meanwhile, steam the broccoli in a steamer basket over 1" boiling water until tender, about 10 minutes. In a large bowl, toss together cooked pasta, steamed broccoli, cheese, olive oil, garlic and pepper. Serve immediately.

Serving size: ¼ of recipe (about 1¼ cups noodles and ½ cup broccoli)
Calories: 358
Fat: 13 g

Suggested sides: 10 grapes (34 calories) or 2 small cantaloupe wedges (38 calories).

Italian Bread Zucchini Casserole

Makes 4 servings

2 tsp. extra-virgin olive oil

3 C. sliced onion

6 (½" thick) slices diagonally-cut Italian bread, toasted

2 (14.5 oz.) cans no-salt-added diced tomatoes, undrained

½ tsp. dried basil

½ tsp. dried thyme

½ tsp. pepper, divided

6 cloves garlic, divided

1 lb. zucchini, halved lengthwise and sliced thin

1¾ C. shredded part-skim mozzarella cheese

1 (15.75 oz.) can low-sodium chicken broth

½ C. fat-free mayonnaise

½ tsp. salt

1 (7 oz.) bottle roasted red bell peppers, drained

Preheat the oven to 375°. Heat the oil in large skillet over medium-high heat. Add the onion; sauté until golden brown, about 15 minutes. Meanwhile, cut the bread into 1" cubes; set aside. Drain the tomatoes, reserving ½ cup liquid. In a medium bowl, combine the tomatoes, basil, thyme and ¼ teaspoon pepper. Mince 3 of the garlic cloves and add to tomatoes. Place ½ cup of the sautéed onions in the bottom of a 2-quart baking dish sprayed with non-stick cooking spray; top with ⅓ of the bread cubes followed by the remaining onion. Top with half of the tomato mixture, half of the zucchini, then half of the cheese. Repeat layers with another ⅓ bread cubes, remaining tomato and remaining zucchini. Top with the remaining bread cubes. Pour the reserved tomato liquid over the casserole. Cover and bake for 30 minutes. Uncover and bake for an additional 25 minutes or until the topping begins to brown.

Serving size: *¼ of recipe (about 2 cups)*
Calories: *387*
Fat: *12.4 g*

Suggested sides: *¼ cup steamed broccoli (13 calories) or 4 steamed asparagus spears (13 calories).*

Parmesan Spinach Bake

8 oz. uncooked
mostaccioli tubular-
shaped pasta
2 T. reduced-calorie
margarine, divided
1 C. sliced onion
2 tsp. minced garlic
¼ C. flour
2½ C. skim milk
1¼ C. plus 2 T. shredded
Parmesan cheese,
divided

1½ tsp. Italian seasoning
½ tsp. pepper
1 (14.5 oz.) can diced
tomatoes with
basil, garlic and
oregano, drained
1 (10 oz.) pkg. frozen
chopped spinach,
thawed and drained
¼ C. dry breadcrumbs

Preheat the oven to 350°. Cook pasta in a large pot of boiling, lightly salted water for 8 to 10 minutes, or until al dente; drain and set aside. Melt 1 tablespoon margarine in a medium saucepan over medium-high heat. Stir onion and garlic into saucepan; sauté for 5 minutes, or until tender. Add flour, stirring constantly for 30 seconds. Gradually stir in milk; cook for 4 minutes or until bubbly. Remove from heat and stir in ¼ cup cheese, Italian seasoning and pepper; set aside. In a large bowl, combine cooked pasta, melted cheese mixture, another 1 cup cheese, drained tomatoes and spinach; mix well. Spread mixture in an even layer into a 9 x 13" baking dish sprayed with non-stick cooking spray. In a small bowl, combine breadcrumbs, remaining 2 tablespoons cheese and remaining 1 tablespoon margarine; sprinkle over casserole. Bake casserole for 30 minutes or until heated through.

Serving size: *⅙ of recipe (about 1½ cups)*
Calories: *372*
Fat: *10.6 g*

Suggested side: *2 cups shredded romaine lettuce sprinkled with 1 tablespoon balsamic vinegar (26 calories).*

Rotini with Spicy Tomato Sauce

1 (12 oz.) pkg. uncooked rotini pasta
1 T. vegetable oil
1 clove garlic, crushed
1 tsp. dried basil
1 tsp. Italian seasoning
1 onion, diced
2 red chile peppers, seeded and chopped
1 (14.5 oz.) can no-salt-added diced tomatoes, undrained
3 drops hot sauce
Salt and pepper to taste

Cook pasta in a large pot of boiling, lightly salted water for 8 to 10 minutes, or until al dente; drain and set aside. Meanwhile, heat the oil in a large skillet or saucepan over medium heat. Add the garlic, basil and Italian seasoning; sauté for 2 to 3 minutes. Stir in the onion and chile peppers; sauté until tender. Add the tomatoes with liquid and the hot sauce; cover and simmer for 5 minutes, or until heated through. Add the cooked pasta to the skillet. Season with salt and pepper to taste and toss until well combined.

Serving size: *⅙ of recipe (about 1 cup pasta and sauce combined)*
Calories: *134*
Fat: *2.8 g*

Suggested sides: *Broccoli Garden Toss (45.5 calories, page 102) and bake up a batch of Pillsbury Frozen Garlic Dinner Rolls; 140 calories per roll.*

Cheesy Prosciutto Lasagna

12 uncooked large lasagna noodles
5 cloves garlic
1 (16 oz.) carton 1% low-fat cottage cheese
½ C. fat-free cream cheese (4 oz.)
¼ C. grated Romano cheese, divided
2½ tsp. dried basil
½ tsp. crushed red pepper flakes
1 large egg
1 (26 oz.) jar fat-free tomato basil pasta sauce
1 C. chopped prosciutto or ham (4 oz.)
1 C. shredded part-skim mozzarella cheese

Preheat the oven to 375°. Cook the lasagna noodles in a large pot of boiling, lightly salted water for 8 to 10 minutes, or until al dente; drain and set aside. In a food processor, pulse the garlic cloves until minced. Add the cottage cheese; process for 2 minutes or until smooth. Add the cream cheese, 2 tablespoons Romano cheese, basil, red pepper flakes and egg. Process until well blended; set aside. Spread ½ cup of the pasta sauce across the bottom of a 9 x 13" baking dish sprayed with non-stick cooking spray. Arrange 3 noodles over the sauce; top with 1 cup of the cheese mixture, ⅓ cup prosciutto, then ¾ cup pasta sauce. Repeat the layers two more times, ending with the noodles. Spread the remaining pasta sauce over the noodles. Sprinkle the remaining Romano and all the mozzarella over the lasagna. Cover and bake for 45 minutes, or until the sauce is bubbly. Uncover and bake for an additional 15 minutes.

Serving size: ⅑ *of recipe (one 3" x 4" rectangle of lasagna)*
Calories: 272
Fat: 5.6 g
Suggested side: Make your own tossed salad. Combine 1 cup spinach plus a few carrot strips and 5 cherry tomatoes (about 30 calories), then toss with your favorite fat-free dressing (about 20 to 50 calories per tablespoon).

Leftovers? You can freeze individual portions of lasagna in freezer-safe bags or containers. To reheat, thaw the frozen portions in the refrigerator for 1 day, then reheat them in a baking dish in a 350° oven until heated through and the cheese is bubbly.

Whole-Wheat Spaghetti with Sautéed Summer Vegetables

Makes 4 servings

8 oz. uncooked whole-wheat spaghetti

1 slice day-old whole-grain bread

2½ T. extra-virgin olive oil, divided

4 cloves garlic, thinly sliced

1½ T. finely chopped walnuts

¼ C. chopped fresh parsley

1 tsp. salt, divided

1 small yellow squash, julienne cut into 2" slices

1 small zucchini, julienne cut into 2" slices

1 C. shredded carrots

1 small red bell pepper, seeded and julienne cut into strips

½ small yellow bell pepper, seeded and diced

½ tsp. pepper

Cook pasta in a large pot of boiling, lightly salted water for 8 to 10 minutes, or until al dente; drain and set aside. In a blender or food processor, process bread until fine crumbs form; set aside. Heat 1½ teaspoons oil in a large skillet over medium heat. Add sliced garlic and sauté until lightly golden, about 1 minute. Stir bread crumbs into skillet and heat until lightly browned and crunchy, about 3 to 4 minutes. Transfer crumb and garlic mixture to a small bowl; stir in walnuts, parsley and ½ teaspoon salt. Set aside walnut mixture. Add remaining 2 tablespoons oil to skillet over medium-high heat. Add squash, zucchini and carrots; sauté until tender but crisp, about 5 minutes. Transfer vegetables to a plate and keep warm. Add bell peppers to skillet; sauté for 2 minutes, or until peppers begin to soften. Stir in remaining ½ teaspoon salt and pepper. Return vegetables to skillet and toss until well mixed; set aside and keep warm. In a shallow serving bowl, combine spaghetti, vegetables and crumb mixture; toss gently to mix and serve immediately.

Serving size: *¼ of recipe (about ¾ cup spaghetti and ½ cup vegetables)*
Calories: *353*
Fat: *12 g*

Suggested side: *Mix-ins for your spaghetti! Add 2 tablespoons canned spaghetti sauce (46 calories), 2 tablespoons grated Parmesan cheese (44 calories), ⅓ cup cooked and diced skinless boneless chicken (44 calories) or 2 tablespoons cooked and crumbled turkey sausage (47 calories).*

Pasta Salad with Spinach & Tuna

2 C. uncooked bow tie pasta

2 (6 oz.) cans unsalted white chunk tuna in water, drained

¼ C. finely chopped green onions

⅔ C. frozen peas, thawed

⅔ C. reduced-fat creamy salad dressing

⅛ tsp. pepper

4 C. fresh spinach

Cook pasta in a large pot of boiling, lightly salted water for 8 to 10 minutes, or until al dente; drain and rinse under cold water. In a large bowl, combine the pasta, tuna, green onions, peas, salad dressing and pepper; toss until well mixed. Cover and chill in the refrigerator at least 2 hours. To serve, place 1 cup of spinach on each of four serving plates. Top each serving with ¼ of the tuna salad.

Serving size: ¼ *of recipe (1 cup spinach and 1 cup tuna salad)*
Calories: *337*
Fat: *15 g*

Suggested side: Stir up a quick fruit salad for four. Dice 1 small peach and mix with 10 halved grapes and 5 large chopped strawberries; mix with an 8-ounce carton of plain, fat-free yogurt. Divide into four portions – just 62 calories per serving!

Sausage & Cheddar Breakfast Casserole

Makes 6 servings

12 oz. turkey
   breakfast sausage
2 C. 1% low-fat milk
2 C. egg substitute
1 tsp. dry mustard
¾ tsp. salt
½ tsp. pepper
¼ tsp. cayenne pepper

3 large eggs
16 (1 oz.) slices
   white bread
1 C. shredded reduced-
   fat extra-sharp
   Cheddar cheese
¼ tsp. paprika

Heat a large non-stick skillet over medium-high heat; coat the pan with non-stick cooking spray. Add the sausage to the skillet and cook for 5 minutes or until browned, stirring and breaking sausage to crumble. Remove skillet from heat and set aside to cool. In a large bowl, combine milk, egg substitute, dry mustard, salt, pepper, cayenne pepper and eggs; whisk until well mixed and set aside. Trim the crusts from the bread. Tear the bread into 1" cubes. Stir bread cubes, sausage and cheese into milk mixture; mix until well combined. Pour the mixture into a 9 x 13" baking dish sprayed with non-stick cooking spray. Spread the egg mixture evenly. Sprinkle casserole evenly with paprika; bake for 45 minutes or until the casserole is set. Let stand 10 minutes before cutting into servings.

Serving size: *⅙ of casserole (about 2 cups)*
Calories: *368*
Fat: *13.6 g*

Suggested sides: *½ cup sliced strawberries (26 calories),
1 small peach (31 calories) or ½ cup diced watermelon (23 calories).*

Want extra cream in your coffee? *You can easily shave more calories and fat from this casserole by cutting it into 12 (1 cup) portions, which would be just 184 calories and 6.8 grams of fat per serving, leaving room for other morning-time indulgences.*

Meatless
Meals

Ratatouille

1 T. extra-virgin olive oil
1 medium onion, halved lengthwise and sliced thin
3 cloves garlic, crushed
1 medium eggplant, cubed
2 medium zucchini, halved lengthwise and sliced thin
1 medium red or green bell pepper, seeded and chopped
1 T. tomato paste
1 C. chopped fresh parsley, or mixture of parsley, basil, thyme and oregano
2 (14.5 oz.) cans no-salt-added diced tomatoes, undrained
1 tsp. chili powder or to taste
¼ C. grated Parmesan cheese, divided

Heat the oil in a large skillet over medium-high heat. Add the onion; sauté until softened. Stir in the garlic and heat for 1 minute. Add the eggplant, zucchini, bell pepper and tomato paste; sauté for 8 minutes. Add the herbs and tomatoes with liquid. Cover the skillet, reduce the heat to medium and simmer for 20 to 30 minutes. Remove from heat and season with chili powder. Divide the ratatouille into four bowls or onto four plates. Top each serving with 1 tablespoon cheese.

Serving size: *¼ of recipe (about 2 cups)*
Calories: *174.5*
Fat: *5.4 g*

Suggested sides: *Whole-Wheat Dinner Rolls (132 calories, page 119) or serve Ratatouille over 1 cup cooked spaghetti (224 calories) or 1 cup cooked white rice (205 calories).*

Couscous with Sun-Dried Tomatoes

Makes 4 servings

1 C. dehydrated sun-dried tomatoes

½ C. plus 2 T. uncooked couscous (5 oz.)

1 tsp. extra-virgin olive-oil

3 cloves garlic, pressed

1 bunch green onions, chopped

⅓ C. chopped fresh basil

¼ C. chopped fresh cilantro

Juice of ½ lemon

Salt and pepper to taste

4 oz. portobello mushroom caps, sliced

Soak sun-dried tomatoes in a bowl with 1 cup water for 30 minutes; drain, reserving water. Chop the tomatoes and set aside. Combine reserved water with enough water to make 1½ cups; bring to a boil in a medium saucepan over medium-high heat. Stir the couscous into the boiling water, cover and remove from heat; let sit for 5 minutes. Once all of the liquid has been absorbed, gently fluff couscous with a fork. Spray the skillet with nonstick cooking spray. Heat the olive oil in a medium skillet over medium-high heat; stir in the sun-dried tomatoes, garlic and green onions; sauté for 5 minutes or until the green onions are tender. Stir the basil, cilantro and lemon juice into the skillet; season with salt and pepper. Mix in the mushrooms; continue to cook for 3 to 5 minutes. Toss the mushroom and tomato mixture with the couscous until evenly mixed.

Serving size: *¼ of recipe (about 1¼ cups)*
Calories: *178*
Fat: *2 g*

Suggested sides: *Dilled Carrots (72 calories, page 114) or Cheesy & Easy Twice-Baked Potatoes (169 calories, page 118).*

Couscous with Chickpeas & Roma Tomatoes

Makes 6 servings

1 C. uncooked couscous
1 (15 oz.) can garbanzo beans, rinsed and drained
2 Roma tomatoes, chopped
1 cucumber, chopped
¼ tsp. extra-virgin olive oil
¼ tsp. white vinegar
Garlic powder to taste
Salt and pepper to taste

Bring 1 cup water to a boil in a medium saucepan over medium-high heat. Stir the couscous into the boiling water, cover and remove from heat; let sit for 5 minutes. Once all of the liquid has been absorbed, gently fluff couscous with a fork. Stir the garbanzo beans into the couscous. Add the tomatoes and cucumbers. Mix in the olive oil and vinegar. Season to taste with garlic powder, salt and pepper; toss until well mixed.

Serving size: *⅙ of recipe (about 1¼ cups)*
Calories: *176*
Fat: *1.2 g*

Suggested sides: *Tasty Breaded Brussels (75 calories, page 109) or a side salad with various vegetables and a light dressing.*

Feel the Burn!

Brush up on your tennis or golf game! Just 10 minutes of playing tennis or 18 minutes of playing golf (without a golf cart) will burn off 100 calories.

Potato & Pinto Bean Enchiladas

Makes 6 servings

½ lb. potatoes, peeled and diced
½ tsp. ground cumin
½ tsp. chili powder
½ tsp. salt
1½ tsp. ketchup
½ lb. fresh tomatillos, husks removed
1 small onion, chopped
½ C. coarsely chopped fresh cilantro, divided
12 (6") corn tortillas
1 (15.5 oz.) can pinto beans, drained
1½ C. queso fresco or shredded Monterey Jack cheese,
    divided (6 oz.)

Preheat the oven to 400°. In a large bowl, toss together potatoes, cumin, chili powder, salt and ketchup; mix well. Transfer mixture to an oven-safe baking dish sprayed with nonstick cooking spray. Bake for 20 to 25 minutes or until tender. Meanwhile, boil tomatillos and chopped onion in a pot of water over medium-high heat for 10 minutes. Set aside to cool; drain. Once cool, puree tomatoes, onions and half of the cilantro in a food processor until smooth; set aside. Heat a large nonstick pan over medium heat. Add 1 tortilla to the pan and heat until softened, about 20 seconds per side. Set tortillas aside on a plate and keep warm. Stir the pinto beans, half of the cheese and remaining cilantro into the potato mixture. Fill each tortilla with ¹⁄₁₂ of the potato and bean mixture, roll up and place seam side down into a 9 x 13" baking dish sprayed with nonstick cooking spray. Spoon the tomatillo sauce over the enchiladas and sprinkle the remaining cheese over top. Bake for 20 minutes or until hot and bubbly.

Serving size: *2 enchiladas*
Calories: *249*
Fat: *5.5 g*

Suggested sides: *Black Beans & Rice (135 calories, page 116) or make your own Baked Tortilla Chips (56 calories per serving, see page 86).*

Southwestern
Soft Tacos

Makes 4 servings

1 T. extra-virgin olive oil
1 medium red onion, chopped
1 C. diced yellow summer squash
1 C. diced zucchini
3 large cloves garlic, minced
4 medium tomatoes, seeded and chopped
1 jalapeno pepper, seeded and chopped
1 C. fresh or frozen corn kernels
1 C. canned pinto or black beans, rinsed and drained
½ C. chopped fresh cilantro
8 (6") corn tortillas
½ C. salsa, divided

Heat the oil in a large skillet over medium heat. Add the onion and sauté until softened. Stir in the squash and zucchini; continue sautéing until vegetables are tender, about 5 minutes. Stir in the garlic, tomatoes, jalapeno, corn and beans. Mix in the cilantro and remove from heat. Heat a large nonstick pan over medium heat. Add 1 tortilla to the pan and heat until softened, about 20 seconds per side. Place 2 tortillas on each serving plate. Top each tortilla with ⅛ of the vegetable and bean mixture. Top each taco with 1 tablespoon salsa. Serve immediately.

Serving size: 2 tacos
Calories: 295
Fat: 4 g

Suggested sides: Corn on the Cob with a light sprinkling of salt (about 60 calories per ear) or a quick fruit salad for four (62 calories per serving, see page 21).

Simple Avocado Tacos

Makes 6 servings

12 (6") corn tortillas
3 avocados, peeled, pitted and mashed
¼ C. diced red onion
¼ tsp. garlic salt
¾ C. chopped fresh cilantro, divided
Hot sauce to taste

Preheat the oven to 325°. Arrange the tortillas in a single layer on a large baking sheet. Bake in the oven for 2 to 5 minutes or until the tortillas are soft, heated and pliable. Meanwhile, in a medium bowl, combine the avocados, onions and garlic salt; set aside. Spread $\frac{1}{12}$ of the avocado mixture over each tortilla. Sprinkle each with 2 tablespoons cilantro and a few drops of hot sauce.

Serving size: *2 tacos*
Calories: *282*
Fat: *16.8 g*

Suggested side: *Whip up a quick batch of Spanish Rice. Cook 3 cups of instant white rice (or equivalent to make 6 cups cooked rice) and stir in a 14.5-ounce can of diced tomatoes with green chilies. Each ½-cup serving is 114 calories.*

Black Bean
Veggie Burgers

Makes 4 servings

1 (16 oz.) can black beans, rinsed and drained

½ green bell pepper, seeded and cut into 2″ pieces

½ onion, cut into wedges

3 cloves garlic

1 egg

1 T. chili powder

1 T. cumin

1 tsp. Thai chili sauce or hot sauce

½ C. bread crumbs

4 light hamburger buns

Preheat an outdoor grill to high heat or preheat the oven to 375°. Spray a sheet of aluminum foil with nonstick cooking spray; set aside. In a medium bowl, mash the beans with a fork until thick and pasty. In a food processor, finely chop the bell pepper, onion and garlic; stir into the black beans. In a small bowl, whisk together the egg, chili powder, cumin and chili sauce; fold into the black bean mixture. Mix in the bread crumbs. Shape the mixture into four patties. Place the prepared foil, oil side up, over the preheated grill or on a baking sheet. Place the patties on the foil and grill for 8 minutes on each side or bake for 10 minutes on each side.

Serving size: *1 burger on 1 bun*
Calories: *280*
Fat: *4 g*

Suggested sides: *Guilt-Free Zesty Coleslaw (45 calories, page 110) or Quick Garlic Asparagus (106 calories, page 113).*

Sloppy Janes

1 T. extra-virgin olive oil
½ C. chopped onion
½ C. chopped celery
½ C. chopped carrots
½ C. seeded and chopped green bell pepper
1 clove garlic, minced
1 (14.5 oz.) can no-salt-added diced tomatoes, undrained
1½ T. chili powder
1 T. tomato paste
1 T. white vinegar
1 tsp. pepper
1 (15 oz.) can kidney beans, rinsed and drained
8 Kaiser rolls

Heat the oil in a large skillet over medium heat. Add the onion, celery, carrot, bell pepper and garlic; sauté until tender. Stir in the tomatoes with liquid, chili powder, tomato paste, vinegar and pepper. Cover skillet, reduce heat and simmer for 10 minutes. Stir in beans and heat for an additional 5 minutes. Cut ¼" slice off the top of each roll; set aside. Hollow out the center of each roll, leaving ½" thick shell. Set aside the removed bread for another use. Spoon the bean and veggie mixture into each roll and replace the tops. Serve immediately.

Serving size: *1 stuffed roll*
Calories: *205*
Fat: *3.9*

Suggested sides: *Guilt-Free Zesty Coleslaw (45 calories, page 110) or Seasoned Green Beans & Cherry Tomatoes (122 calories, page 112).*

Brown Rice, Lentils & Veggie Bake

Makes 4 servings

½ C. uncooked long grain white rice

1 C. red lentils

1 tsp. vegetable oil

1 small onion, chopped

3 cloves garlic, minced

1 large tomato, chopped

⅓ C. chopped celery

⅓ C. chopped carrots

⅓ C. chopped zucchini

1 (8 oz.) can tomato sauce, divided

1 tsp. dried basil, divided

1 tsp. dried oregano, divided

1 tsp. ground cumin, divided

Salt and pepper to taste

Place the rice and 1 cup water in a pot over medium-high heat; bring to a boil. Cover the pot, reduce the heat to low and simmer for 20 minutes. Place the lentils in a separate pot with 1½ cups water; bring to a boil and cook for 15 minutes, or until tender. Preheat the oven to 350°. Heat the oil in a large skillet over medium heat. Add the onion and garlic; sauté for 2 minutes. Stir in the tomato, celery, carrots, zucchini and half of the tomato sauce. Season with ½ teaspoon basil, ½ teaspoon oregano, ½ teaspoon cumin, salt and pepper. Continue to cook and stir until vegetables are tender. In a 2-quart baking dish, combine the rice, drained lentils and sautéed vegetables. Pour the remaining tomato sauce over the mixture. Top with the remaining basil, oregano and cumin. Bake, uncovered, for 30 minutes, or until heated through and bubbly.

Serving size: ¼ of recipe (about 1 cup)
Calories: 285
Fat: 2.25 g

Suggested sides: Balsamic Mandarin Salad (74 calories, page 101) or 1 (0.3 oz.) package of sugar-free gelatin prepared with 8 large sliced strawberries (about 20 calories per 1-cup serving).

Microwave Veggie Wrap

Makes 6 servings

1 (15.5 oz.) can black beans, rinsed and drained
1¼ C. frozen corn kernels, thawed
3 T. chopped fresh cilantro
2 T. seeded and chopped green chili peppers
4 green onions, diced
1 tomato, diced
1 T. minced garlic
6 (10") fat-free tortillas
¾ C. shredded low-fat or fat-free Cheddar cheese
¾ C. salsa

In a microwave-safe bowl, combine the black beans, corn, cilantro, chili peppers, green onions, tomato and garlic; mix well. Microwave beans and vegetables for 45 seconds. Stir and heat for an additional 45 seconds. Repeat until mixture is hot. Place 2 tortillas between paper towels and heat in the microwave for 20 seconds; repeat with remaining tortillas. To serve, place ½ cup of the bean mixture on each tortilla. Top each with 2 tablespoons cheese and 2 tablespoons salsa. Fold the sides and bottom of the tortillas over the filling, then roll to close.

Serving size: *1 sandwich wrap*
Calories: *330*
Fat: *9 g*

Suggested sides: *1 large watermelon wedge (about 70 calories), 1 large cantaloupe wedge (about 35 calories) or 20 large grapes (about 70 calories).*

Grilled Focaccia Sandwiches

¼ C. reduced-fat mayonnaise

3 cloves garlic, minced

1 T. lemon juice

2 T. extra-virgin olive oil

1 C. seeded and sliced red bell peppers

1 small zucchini, sliced

1 red onion, sliced

1 small yellow squash, sliced

2 (4 x 6") focaccia bread pieces, split horizontally

½ C. crumbled reduced-fat feta cheese

In a small bowl, combine the mayonnaise, garlic and lemon juice; set aside in the refrigerator. Preheat an outdoor grill to high heat and lightly brush the grate with oil. Brush the peppers, zucchini, onion and squash pieces with oil. Place the pepper and zucchini pieces closest to the middle of the grill and surround them with the onion and squash pieces. Grill the vegetables for 3 minutes on each side. Remove the vegetables from the grill and set aside. Spread some of the mayonnaise mixture over each cut side of the bread. Sprinkle 2 tablespoons feta cheese over each bread half. Place the bread on the grill, cheese side up, cover and heat for 2 to 3 minutes or until the cheese is slightly melted. Divide the grilled vegetables evenly and place some of each kind over the cheese on each bread half. Serve as open-faced sandwiches.

Serving size: *1 open-faced sandwich*
Calories: *324*
Fat: *15.6 g*

Suggested sides: *1 medium apple (72 calories) or ½ of a large banana (60 calories).*

Tomato & Parmesan Eggplant Bake

Makes 8 servings

3 large eggplants, cut into ¼" slices
1½ tsp. salt
1 T. extra-virgin olive oil
2 onions, chopped
2 cloves garlic, crushed
1 tsp. dried basil
1 tsp. dried oregano
1 (10.75 oz.) can tomato puree
Pinch of pepper
2 (8 oz.) containers low-fat plain yogurt
¼ C. wheat germ or whole-wheat bread crumbs
2 T. grated Parmesan cheese

Sprinkle the eggplant slices lightly with salt; set aside for 30 minutes. Heat the oil in a large skillet over low heat. Add the onions and garlic; cover and sauté until tender and the onions are golden. Stir in the basil, oregano, tomato puree, pepper and ¼ cup water; simmer for 10 minutes. Rinse off the eggplant slices and place in a steamer basket over boiling water for about 10 minutes, working in batches as needed. Preheat the oven to 350°. Spray a 9 x 13" baking dish with non-stick cooking spray. Spread about 3 tablespoons of the tomato mixture over the bottom of the dish; top with ⅓ of the eggplant slices. Cover the eggplant with ⅓ of the remaining tomato mixture; top with 1 container of yogurt. Repeat layers with another eggplant layer, ⅓ of the sauce, 1 container of yogurt, remaining eggplant, and finish with the remaining tomato mixture. Cover the dish with foil and bake for 30 minutes. Uncover and sprinkle with wheat germ and Parmesan cheese; bake for 20 to 30 minutes or until the topping is golden brown.

Serving size: *⅛ of recipe (one 3 x 4" rectangle)*
Calories: *147*
Fat: *3.6 g*
Suggested sides: *Low-Fat Potato Salad (206 calories, page 104) or Whole-Wheat Dinner Rolls (132 calories, page 119).*

Orange Stir-Fry

¼ C. plus 1 T. vegetable oil, divided
¼ C. plus 1 tsp. cornstarch, divided
1 (16 oz.) pkg. firm tofu, drained and cut into strips
2 T. soy sauce
½ C. orange juice
1 T. sugar
1 tsp. chili paste
2 carrots, sliced

Heat ¼ cup oil in a wok or non-stick skillet over medium-high heat. Place ¼ cup cornstarch in a shallow dish. Press the tofu slices in the cornstarch to coat all sides. Stir-fry the tofu pieces for 5 minutes, or until golden brown on all sides. Drain the tofu on paper towels. Let the wok cool and wipe clean with a paper towel. In a medium bowl, combine the soy sauce, orange juice, ¼ cup warm water, sugar, chili paste and remaining 1 teaspoon cornstarch until smooth. Heat the remaining 1 tablespoon oil in the wok or skillet. Add the carrots; stir-fry until tender. Form a well in the center of the carrots. Pour the sauce mixture into the well; bring to a boil. Mix the tofu into the wok and continue cooking until all pieces are coated in the sauce.

Serving size: *¼ of recipe (about 1¼ cups)*
Calories: *286*
Fat: *15 g*

Suggested side: *½ cup cooked white rice (103 calories).*

Cheesy Mushroom Omelet

Makes 2 servings

1 T. extra-virgin olive oil
4 large fresh mushrooms, sliced
1 T. seeded and chopped jalapeno pepper
¼ tsp. dried basil
4 eggs, beaten
¼ C. low-fat 1% cottage cheese
Pepper to taste

Heat the oil in a medium skillet over medium heat. Add the mushrooms and jalapeno; sauté until softened. Sprinkle basil over vegetables; mix well and transfer to a plate. Pour eggs into pan and return to heat. Cook eggs until almost cooked through, then flip over. Place mushroom mixture and cottage cheese over half of the omelet circle; season with pepper. Fold half of the omelet over the filling to make a half circle. Cook until eggs are firm. Cut omelet in half.

Serving size: *½ of recipe (½ of a large omelet)*
Calories: *250*
Fat: *18.3 g*

Suggested sides: *2 small (4") pancakes prepared from a dry mix with sugar-free, no-calorie syrup as a topper (about 150 calories).*

Feel the Burn!

Frisbee anyone? Just under 40 minutes of leisurely throwing the disk will result in 150 calories burned!

Brown Rice, Swiss & Spinach Quiche

Makes 8 servings

1½ C. cooked brown rice

1 C. shredded reduced-fat Swiss cheese, divided

¾ C. egg substitute, divided

¼ tsp. curry powder

1 (10 oz.) pkg. frozen chopped spinach, thawed and drained

¾ C. fat-free evaporated milk

½ C. sliced fresh mushrooms

2 T. chopped onion

¼ tsp. garlic powder

⅛ tsp. pepper

In a medium bowl, combine the prepared rice, ½ cup cheese, ¼ cup egg substitute and curry powder; mix well and press into the bottom and up the sides of a 9" microwave-safe pie plate. Microwave on high for 4 to 5 minutes or until firm. In the same bowl, combine the spinach, evaporated milk, mushrooms, onion, garlic powder, pepper, remaining ½ cup cheese and remaining ½ cup egg substitute; mix well and pour into the rice crust. Microwave on 50% power for 20 minutes, rotating every 5 minutes if microwave does not have a turntable. The quiche is done when a knife inserted in the center comes out clean.

Serving size: *1 quiche wedge (⅛ of pie)*
Calories: *116*
Fat: *2 g*

Suggested sides: *Rosemary Roasted Potatoes (227 calories, page 107), 1 regular (8-ounce) glass of orange juice (112 calories) or 1 large orange (86 calories).*

Meat & Poultry

Texas Steak & Peppers

Makes 4 servings

½ tsp. ground cumin
½ tsp. ground coriander
½ tsp. chili powder
¼ tsp. salt
¾ tsp. pepper
1 lb. boneless top sirloin steak, trimmed of fat
3 cloves garlic, 1 halved, 2 minced
1 T. extra-virgin olive oil, divided

2 red bell peppers, seeded and thinly sliced
1 medium onion, halved lengthwise and thinly sliced
1 tsp. brown sugar
½ C. brewed coffee
¼ C. balsamic vinegar
4 C. watercress sprigs

In a small bowl, combine cumin, coriander, chili powder, salt and pepper. Rub steak with cut garlic halves and rub with the spice mix. Heat 2 teaspoons of oil in a large heavy skillet over medium-high heat. Add the steak and cook to desired doneness, about 4 to 6 minutes per side for medium-rare. Transfer the steak to a cutting board and let rest. Add the remaining 1 teaspoon oil to the skillet. Stir in the bell peppers and onion; sauté until softened, about 4 minutes. Add the minced garlic and brown sugar; heat for 1 minute. Stir in the coffee, vinegar and any accumulated meat juices from the cutting board; heat for 3 minutes, then season with additional pepper to taste. To serve, mound 1 cup watercress on each of four plates. Top each with some of the sautéed peppers and onion. Slice the steak across the grain and arrange on the vegetables. Pour the sauce from the pan over the steak.

Serving size: *1 cup watercress, ¼ cup peppers and ¼ pound steak*
Calories: *226*
Fat: *9 g*

Suggested sides: *Quinoa with Black Beans (154 calories, page 106) or Scalloped Corn & Broccoli (162 calories, page 111).*

Beef with Spicy Gravy

Makes 6 servings

1 T. unsweetened cocoa
1 T. ground coriander
1½ tsp. garlic powder
1½ tsp. ground cumin
1½ tsp. ancho
   chile powder
1½ tsp. paprika
1½ tsp. dried oregano
⅛ tsp. ground cinnamon
1½ lbs. top round steak,
   trimmed of fat and cut
   into 1" cubes
½ C. flour

1 T. extra-virgin olive oil
½ C. chopped onion
½ C. seeded and
   chopped green
   bell pepper
½ C. dry red wine
1 (14.5 oz.) can diced
   fire-roasted tomatoes,
   undrained
2 C. low-sodium
   beef broth
1 tsp. salt
⅛ tsp. pepper

In a large bowl, combine the cocoa, coriander, garlic powder, cumin, chile powder, paprika, oregano and cinnamon. Add the beef cubes to the bowl, tossing until well coated. Remove beef cubes from the bowl. Stir the flour into the remaining dry mix in the bowl, stirring with a whisk. Return the beef to the bowl, tossing to coat. Heat the oil in a large Dutch oven or pot over medium-high heat. Add the beef cubes to the pan; sauté for 5 minutes, turning to brown all sides. Remove the beef to a plate and keep warm. Add the onion and bell pepper to the pan; sauté for 5 minutes, or until tender. Stir the red wine and tomatoes with liquid into the pan. Cover, reduce heat and let simmer for 1 hour, or until the beef is tender, stirring occasionally. Divide the beef cubes into six portions, spooning an even amount of the sauce over each portion.

Serving size: about 1 cup beef cubes and ¼ cup gravy sauce
Calories: 263
Fat: 7.8 g

Suggested sides: Stuffed Zucchini Boats (107 calories, page 105) or Mashed Turnip & Potatoes (100 calories, page 108).

Easy Beef Enchiladas

Makes 4 servings

½ lb. extra-lean ground beef
½ C. seeded and chopped green bell pepper
½ C. seeded and chopped red bell pepper
2 C. thick n' chunky salsa, divided
1 C. reduced-fat 2% sharp Cheddar cheese, divided
2 T. reduced-fat light zesty Italian dressing
8 (6") corn tortillas
2 T. chopped fresh cilantro

Preheat oven to 400°. In a large non-stick skillet over medium heat, cook the ground beef and bell peppers until the beef is no longer pink, stirring often. Drain the grease from the skillet. Stir in 1 cup salsa and simmer for 3 to 4 minutes or until the peppers are tender. Remove from heat and stir in ½ cup cheese. Spread ¼ cup of the salsa across the bottom of a 9 x 13" baking dish. Brush the dressing lightly over both sides of the tortillas. Wrap the tortillas in waxed paper and microwave on high for 20 to 30 seconds or until warmed. Immediately spoon ⅓ cup meat mixture down the center of each tortilla; roll up and place seam side down in the baking dish. Repeat with the remaining tortillas and meat mixture. Spoon the remaining ¾ cup salsa evenly over the tortillas. Cover the dish with aluminum foil. Bake for 20 minutes or until heated through. Uncover and top with the remaining ½ cup cheese; bake for an additional 2 to 3 minutes or until the cheese is melted. Sprinkle with the cilantro.

Serving size: *2 enchiladas*
Calories: *340*
Fat: *11 g*

Suggested sides: *Baked Tortilla Chips (56 calories per serving, see page 86) or ¼ cup of canned heated black beans or pinto beans (60 calories).*

Herbed Rice Meatloaf

Makes 4 servings

1 lb. extra-lean ground beef

½ C. uncooked instant white rice

¼ C. finely chopped onion

¼ C. seeded and minced red bell pepper

1 clove garlic, minced

1 tsp. salt

1 tsp. pepper

1 T. minced fresh herbs, such as rosemary, basil, chives or sage

2 tsp. Worcestershire sauce

1 egg, beaten

¼ C. ketchup

¼ C. skim milk

¼ C. dry bread crumbs

Preheat the oven to 350°. Spray a 5 x 9" loaf pan with nonstick cooking spray. In a large bowl, combine beef, uncooked rice, onion, bell pepper, garlic, salt, pepper, herbs, Worcestershire sauce, egg, ketchup, milk and bread crumbs. Mix by hand until well combined, being careful not to over-mix. Shape the mixture into a loaf shape without packing too tightly. Place in the loaf pan; bake for 60 minutes or until the internal temperature of the loaf is 160°. Remove from the oven and let sit for 15 minutes before serving.

Serving size: *2 (1"-thick) slices meatloaf*
Calories: *347*
Fat: *7.3 g*

Suggested sides: *10 steamed baby carrots (40 calories) or 6 steamed broccoli florets (48 calories).*

Blue Ribbon Meatloaf

Makes 6 servings

2 tsp. canola oil
1 medium sweet onion, chopped
1 (12 oz.) bottle dark or amber beer
1 tsp. dried thyme
1 tsp. dry mustard
¾ tsp. salt
Pepper to taste

1¼ lbs. extra lean ground beef
1¼ lbs. 93% lean ground turkey
1 C. whole-wheat bread crumbs
¼ C. chopped fresh parsley
1 large egg, lightly beaten
1 egg white, lightly beaten

Preheat the oven to 375°. Spray a 5 x 9" loaf pan with nonstick cooking spray; set aside. Heat the oil in a large nonstick skillet over medium-high heat. Add the onion; sauté until softened and starting to brown, about 5 minutes. Add the beer and increase the heat to high. Bring to a rapid boil, cooking until the liquid is syrupy and reduces to about ¾ cup, about 8 to 10 minutes. Transfer the mixture to a large bowl. Stir in the thyme, dry mustard, salt and pepper; let cool for 10 minutes. Mix in the beef, turkey, bread crumbs, parsley, egg and egg white by hand until well combined, being careful not to over-mix. Shape the mixture into a loaf shape without packing too tightly. Place in the loaf pan; bake for 60 minutes or until the internal temperature of the loaf is 160°. Remove from the oven and let sit for 15 minutes before serving.

Serving size: 1 (1½"-thick) slice meatloaf
Calories: 366
Fat: 17.3 g
Suggested side: Instead of serving the standard mashed potatoes with your meatloaf, whip up some mashed garlic cauliflower. Simply chop a head of cauliflower into small flowerets; steam over boiling water until tender. Transfer the steamed cauliflower to a bowl; add ¼ cup of skim milk and 1 teaspoon of garlic powder; mash to desired texture. Divide into four portions. Each portion is only 23 calories and packed with flavor!

Chipotle Pulled Pork

Makes 12 servings

1 T. extra-virgin olive oil
2 medium yellow
   onions, diced
2 T. chili powder
1 T. ground cumin
2 tsp. paprika
1 tsp. cayenne pepper
1 (12 oz.) bottle lager beer
¾ C. ketchup

¾ C. cider vinegar
½ C. whole-grain mustard
2 T. low-sodium
   tomato paste
1 canned chipotle pepper
   in adobo sauce, minced,
   plus 1 T. adobo sauce
1 (5 lb.) bone-in pork butt
   or shoulder

Preheat the oven to 300°. Heat oil in a large Dutch oven or pot over medium-low heat. Add onions, stirring occasionally, until lightly browned and very soft, about 20 minutes. Increase heat to high and stir in chili powder, cumin, paprika and cayenne; cook and stir for 1 minute. Mix in beer, ketchup, vinegar, mustard, tomato paste, minced pepper and adobo sauce; bring to a boil. Reduce heat to medium-low and simmer, uncovered, until sauce is slightly thickened, about 10 minutes. Meanwhile, trim all fat from pork. Remove pan from heat and add pork, spooning sauce over top. Cover pot and transfer to oven; bake for 90 minutes. Turn pork over, cover with sauce and bake for an additional 90 minutes. Uncover and bake pork until meat pulls apart easily, another 1 to 2 hours. Transfer pork to a large bowl and cover with foil. Pour sauce from pan into a large measuring cup; refrigerate for 15 minutes, or until the fat separates from the sauce. Skim off fat. Return sauce to pan and heat over medium-high heat for about 4 minutes. Shred pork meat, discarding any fat or bone, with two forks. Mix sauce into shredded meat, stirring until well combined.

Serving size: *about 3 ounces (⅓ cup) pulled pork*
Calories: *281*
Fat: *14 g*

Suggested side: *Want to serve this pulled pork on buns? Choose wisely! Some buns are more than 300 calories apiece. Wonder Lite Hamburger Buns and Nature's Own Double Fiber Wheat Buns bake up to just 80 calories each, and Pepperidge Farm Classic Whole-Grain White Buns are just 100 calories per bun.*

Citrus Glazed
Pork Tenderloin

Makes 6 servings

½ C. kosher salt
½ C. sugar
2 (1 lb.) pork tenderloins, trimmed of fat
½ C. orange juice concentrate, thawed
3 large cloves garlic, minced
2 tsp. Italian seasoning

Dissolve the salt and sugar in a bowl with 4 cups of water. Add the meat to the bowl and let stand for 45 minutes. Rinse the meat, then pat dry. Preheat an outdoor grill to high heat and lightly oil the grate. Meanwhile, place the orange juice concentrate in a small saucepan over low heat; cook until reduced by half. Stir in the garlic and Italian seasoning. Brush the glaze over the pork. Place the tenderloins on the hot grill rack and close the lid; grill for about 7 minutes or until well-seared. Turn the pork over and grill the second side for about 6 minutes. Turn off the grill and let the tenderloins sit in the covered grill until the internal temperature of the pork is 160°.

Serving size: *about 5 to 6 ounces pork tenderloin*
Calories: *263*
Fat: *5.5 g*

Suggested sides: *Seasoned Green Beans & Cherry Tomatoes (122 calories, page 112) or Spiced Brown Rice with Corn (133 calories, page 117).*

Quick Pork Chops Supreme

4 pork loin or rib chops, about ¾" thick
Salt and pepper to taste
1 small onion, cut into ¼" thick slices
1 large lemon, cut into ¼" thick slices
¼ C. brown sugar
¼ C. ketchup, chili sauce or barbecue sauce

Preheat the oven to 350°. Sprinkle both sides of the pork chops with salt and pepper. Place the pork chops in an ungreased baking sheet with a rimmed edge. Top each pork chop with ¼ of the onion slices, ¼ of the lemon slices, 1 tablespoon brown sugar and 1 tablespoon ketchup. Cover the baking sheet and cook the pork chops for about 20 minutes. Uncover the pork, spoon the pan juices over the chops, and bake for an additional 30 minutes, or until the internal temperature of the pork is 160°.

Serving size: *1 pork chop plus ¼ of the onions and sauce (about ¼ cup)*
Calories: *157*
Fat: *3 g*

Suggested sides: *Rosemary Roasted Potatoes (227 calories, page 107) or Corn Bread Custard (168 calories, page 120).*

Maple & Mustard Pork Tenderloin

Makes 4 servings

3 T. Dijon mustard, divided
½ tsp. kosher salt
½ tsp. pepper
1 lb. pork tenderloin, trimmed of fat
2 tsp. canola oil
¼ C. cider vinegar
2 T. maple syrup
1½ tsp. chopped fresh sage

Preheat the oven to 475°. In a small bowl, combine 1 tablespoon mustard, salt and pepper; rub over pork. Heat the oil in a large oven-safe skillet over medium-high heat. Add the pork to the skillet and brown on all sides. Transfer the skillet with pork to the oven; roast until the internal temperature of the pork is 160°. Remove the pork from the oven and transfer to a cutting board; let rest for 5 minutes. Place the same skillet over medium-high heat. Add the vinegar to the skillet and bring to a boil, scraping up any browned bits from the bottom of the skillet. Whisk in the maple syrup and remaining 2 tablespoons mustard; return to a boil. Reduce the heat to medium-low and let simmer until the sauce thickens, about 5 minutes; stir in sage. Slice the pork. Divide the pork slices into four portions. Top each portion with ¼ of the sauce.

Serving size: *about 4 ounces sliced pork and ¼ of the sauce (about 1 to 2 tablespoons)*
Calories: *227*
Fat: *8 g*

Suggested sides: *Quick Garlic Asparagus (106 calories, page 113) or Cheesy & Easy Twice-Baked Potatoes (169 calories, page 118).*

Ham & Asparagus Toss

Makes 4 servings

8 oz. whole-wheat bow-tie pasta
1 bunch asparagus, cut into 2" pieces
8 oz. cooked ham, cut into 2" pieces
¼ C. no-fat sour cream
⅓ C. skim milk
2 tsp. dried chives
Pinch of garlic powder
Pinch of onion powder

Cook pasta in a large pot of boiling, lightly salted water for 8 to 10 minutes, or until al dente. Add the asparagus pieces during the last 5 minutes of cooking and add the ham during the last 1 minute of cooking time. Drain the pasta, asparagus and ham; return to the pot. In a glass measuring cup, whisk together the sour cream and skim milk; stir in the chives, garlic powder and onion powder. Pour the sauce mixture over the pasta mixture; toss until evenly coated. Serve immediately.

Serving size: *1½ cups pasta, ham and asparagus mixture*
Calories: *341*
Fat: *2 g*

Suggested sides: *1 cup peach halves or slices canned in water (59 calories) or 15 large grapes (51 calories).*

Feel the Burn!

Burn calories while entertaining friends and family with your sweet piano playing. You'll burn 200 calories for 56 minutes of tickling the ivories.

Ham & Cheese Stuffed Chicken

¼ C. shredded Swiss, Monterey Jack or part-skim mozzarella cheese

2 T. chopped cooked ham

2 tsp. Dijon mustard

Pepper to taste

4 (4 to 4.5 oz. each) boneless, skinless chicken breast halves, trimmed of fat

1 egg white

½ C. dry bread crumbs

2 tsp. extra-virgin olive oil

Preheat the oven to 400°. Lightly spray a rimmed baking sheet with nonstick cooking spray. In a small bowl, combine the cheese, ham, mustard and pepper; mix lightly. Cut a slit horizontally along one side of each chicken breast half, cutting almost but not completely through to the opposite side. Place ¼ of the filling in the center of one chicken breast half. Fold the chicken over the filling, pressing the edges to seal, securing with toothpicks if necessary. In a medium bowl, lightly beat the egg white. Place the bread crumbs in a separate shallow dish. Dip the chicken first into the egg and then into the bread crumbs, turning to coat both sides. Heat the oil in a large nonstick skillet over medium-high heat. Cook the chicken until browned on one side, about 2 minutes. Place the chicken browned side up on the prepared baking sheet; bake for about 20 minutes, or until the chicken is cooked through.

Serving size: *1 stuffed chicken breast half*
Calories: *236*
Fat: *7 g*

Suggested sides: *White Wine Herbed Mushrooms (55 calories, page 115) or Scalloped Corn & Broccoli (162 calories, page 111).*

Cajun Spiced Chicken

Makes 6 servings

¼ C. flour
1½ tsp. salt, divided
Pinch of pepper
6 (4 to 4.5 oz. each) boneless, skinless chicken breast halves, trimmed of fat
3 T. butter
1 (14.5) oz. can no-salt-added stewed tomatoes, undrained
2 T. brown sugar
2 T. white vinegar
2 T. Worcestershire sauce
2 tsp. chili powder
1 tsp. mustard powder
½ tsp. celery seed
1 clove garlic, minced
⅛ tsp. hot sauce

In a shallow dish, combine the flour, ½ teaspoon salt and pepper. Dredge the chicken in the flour mixture, turning to coat both sides. Melt the butter in a large skillet over medium heat. Add the chicken to the skillet and cook for 2 minutes on each side, or until evenly browned. Remove the chicken from the skillet and place on paper towels to drain. In the same skillet over medium heat, combine the tomatoes with liquid, brown sugar, vinegar and Worcestershire sauce. Stir in the remaining 1 teaspoon salt, chili powder, mustard powder, celery seed, garlic and hot sauce. Bring the mixture to a boil, then reduce the heat to medium-low. Return the chicken to the skillet and simmer until cooked through.

Serving size: *1 covered chicken breast half*
Calories: *247*
Fat: *7.7 g*

Suggested sides: *Mashed Turnip & Potatoes (100 calories, page 108) or Black Beans & Rice (135 calories, page 116).*

Sweet & Spicy Pineapple Chicken

Makes 4 servings

4 (4 to 4.5 oz. each) boneless, skinless chicken breast halves, trimmed of fat

Salt and pepper to taste

1 T. extra-virgin olive oil

1 red or yellow bell pepper, seeded and chopped

1 small red onion, chopped

1 jalapeno pepper, seeded and minced

1 or 2 cloves garlic, minced

½ C. low-sodium chicken broth

1 small fresh pineapple, peeled, cored, and chopped

1 T. chopped fresh parsley

Preheat the oven to 375°. Season the chicken with salt and pepper to taste. Sear both sides of the chicken in a large skillet over medium-high heat. Transfer the chicken to a baking sheet and place in the oven. Meanwhile, heat the oil in the same skillet over medium heat. Add the bell pepper, onion, jalapeno and garlic; sauté until softened. Add the chicken broth to the skillet and simmer until most of the liquid has been evaporated and the vegetables have cooked down. Stir in the pineapple and parsley during the last 3 minutes of cooking time. When the chicken is cooked through, about 20 to 25 minutes, transfer one cooked chicken breast half to each serving plate. Divide the pineapple and pepper mixture into four portions and spoon over the chicken on each plate.

Serving size: 1 chicken breast half plus ¼ of the pineapple mixture (about 1 cup)
Calories: 262
Fat: 5.5 g

Suggested sides: Broccoli Garden Toss (45.5 calories, page 102) or Spiced Brown Rice with Corn (133 calories, page 117).

Artichoke Chicken

4 (4 to 4.5 oz. each) boneless, skinless chicken breast halves, trimmed of fat

Salt and pepper to taste

2 tsp. extra-virgin olive oil

1 (14.5 oz.) can diced tomatoes with green pepper and onions, undrained

¼ C. sun-dried tomato pesto

1 (14 oz.) can artichoke hearts in water, drained and quartered

Season both sides of each chicken breast half with salt and pepper. Heat the oil in a large skillet over medium-high heat. Place the chicken in the skillet and cook for about 4 minutes on each side, or until evenly browned. Transfer the chicken to a plate and keep warm. Pour the tomatoes and liquid into the skillet; cook for 1 minute, stirring constantly and scraping up any browned bits from the bottom of the skillet. Stir in the pesto and artichokes. Return the chicken to the pan, cover and reduce the heat to medium. Simmer for 5 to 10 minutes, or until the chicken is cooked through.

Serving size: *1 chicken breast half plus ¼ of the artichoke sauce (about ½ cup)*
Calories: *249*
Fat: *6.5 g*

Suggested sides: *Spiced Grape Salad (70 calories, page 103) or Stuffed Zucchini Boats (107 calories, page 105).*

Spice Rack Chicken

Makes 4 servings

1 C. nonfat plain yogurt
1 small onion, minced
2 cloves garlic, minced
1½ T. lemon juice
1 tsp. chopped fresh cilantro
½ tsp. paprika
½ tsp. ground cumin
½ tsp. ground turmeric
½ tsp. ground ginger
½ tsp. salt
¼ tsp. pepper
¼ tsp. ground cinnamon
Pinch of ground cloves
4 (3 oz. each) skinless, bone-in chicken thighs, trimmed of fat

In a large shallow dish, combine the yogurt, onion and garlic. Stir in the lemon juice, cilantro, paprika, cumin, turmeric, ginger, salt, pepper, cinnamon and cloves. Add the chicken thighs to the mixture, turning to coat all sides. Cover the dish and chill in the refrigerator for 2 hours or overnight to marinate. Preheat the oven to 500°. Coat a wire rack with cooking spray and set it over a foil- or parchment-covered baking sheet. Place the chicken on the prepared rack. Discard the marinade. Bake the chicken until cooked through, about 25 to 30 minutes.

Serving size: *1 chicken thigh*
Calories: *227*
Fat: *5.7 g*

Suggested sides: *Quinoa with Black Beans (154 calories, page 106) or Corn Bread Custard (168 calories, page 120).*

Chicken with Asparagus & Roasted Peppers

Makes 4 servings

½ C. low-sodium chicken broth

4 (4 to 4.5 oz. each) boneless, skinless chicken breast halves, trimmed of fat

Salt and pepper to taste

½ lb. fresh asparagus, trimmed and cut into 2″ pieces

1 (7 oz.) jar roasted red peppers, drained and chopped

1 clove garlic, minced

2 small Roma tomatoes, chopped

1 tsp. balsamic vinegar

½ C. shredded part-skim mozzarella cheese, divided

Heat the broth in a large skillet over medium-high heat. Season both sides of each chicken breast half with salt and pepper; place in the skillet. Cook for 15 minutes, or until the chicken is almost cooked through. Add the asparagus, red peppers and garlic to the skillet. Continue cooking for 10 minutes, or until the chicken is cooked through and the asparagus is tender. Add the tomatoes to the skillet during the last 2 minutes of cooking time. Place one chicken breast half on each of four plates and top each with an even amount of the asparagus, peppers and tomatoes. Sprinkle 2 tablespoons cheese over each serving.

Serving size: 1 chicken breast half plus ¼ of the vegetables (about 1 cup)
Calories: 190
Fat: 5.3 g

Suggested sides: Low-Fat Potato Salad (206 calories, page 104) or Whole-Wheat Dinner Rolls (132 calories, page 119).

Chicken & Shallots in White Wine Sauce

Makes 4 servings

4 (4 to 4.5 oz. each) boneless, skinless chicken breast halves, trimmed of fat

¼ tsp. salt

¼ tsp. pepper

1 T. extra-virgin olive oil, divided

¼ C. finely chopped shallots

½ C. low-sodium chicken broth

½ C. dry white wine

1 T. Dijon mustard

1 T. reduced-fat sour cream

1 T. chopped fresh tarragon

Season both sides of each chicken breast half with salt and pepper. Heat 1½ teaspoons oil in a large skillet over medium-high heat. Add the chicken and cook for 3 minutes on each side, or until well browned. Transfer the chicken to a plate and keep warm. Reduce the heat to medium and add the remaining 1½ teaspoons oil. Add the shallots to the skillet; sauté until softened, about 2 to 3 minutes. Add the broth and wine to the skillet; bring to a simmer. Cook until the liquid is reduced by half. Return the chicken and any juices to the pan; reduce the heat to low. Simmer until the chicken is cooked through, about 4 minutes. Transfer one cooked chicken breast half to each of four plates and keep warm. Stir the mustard, sour cream and tarragon into the sauce in the skillet. Season to taste with additional salt and pepper. Spoon an even amount of the sauce over each serving.

Serving size: 1 chicken breast half plus ¼ of the sauce (about 2 tablespoons)
Calories: 199
Fat: 7 g

Suggested sides: White Wine Herbed Mushrooms (55 calories, page 115) or Cheesy & Easy Twice-Baked Potatoes (169 calories, page 118).

Simple Teriyaki Grilled Chicken

Makes 4 servings

4 (4 to 4.5 oz. each) boneless, skinless chicken breast halves, trimmed of fat

1 C. teriyaki sauce

¼ C. lemon juice

2 tsp. minced garlic

2 tsp. sesame oil

Place the chicken, teriyaki sauce, lemon juice, garlic and oil in a large re-sealable plastic bag. Seal the bag, shaking to coat all the chicken. Place the bag in the refrigerator for 24 hours, turning every few hours. Preheat an outdoor grill to high heat and lightly oil the grate. Remove the chicken from the bag, discarding the marinade. Grill the chicken for 6 to 8 minutes on each side, or until the chicken is cooked through.

Serving size: *1 chicken breast half*
Calories: *160*
Fat: *3.1 g*

Suggested sides: *Rosemary Roasted Potatoes (227 calories, page 107) or Tasty Breaded Brussels (75 calories, page 109).*

Grilled Orange Chicken Fingers

Makes 4 servings

4 (4 to 4.5 oz. each) boneless, skinless chicken breast halves, trimmed of fat

1½ T. Dijon mustard

1½ T. frozen orange juice concentrate, thawed

1½ T. honey

1 tsp. sesame oil

½ tsp. pepper

Salt to taste

Cut the chicken into ¾" wide strips; set aside. In a medium bowl, whisk together the mustard, orange juice concentrate, honey, oil and pepper. Add the chicken to the bowl, tossing until evenly coated. Cover the bowl and place in the refrigerator for 15 minutes to marinate. Meanwhile, preheat an outdoor grill to high heat and lightly oil the grate. Remove the chicken from the bowl, discarding the marinade. Grill the chicken for 4 to 6 minutes on each side, or until the chicken is cooked through.

Serving size: *¼ of the chicken strips (about 3 to 4 strips)*
Calories: *174*
Fat: *4 g*

Suggested sides: *Low-Fat Potato Salad (206 calories, page 104) or Guilt-Free Zesty Coleslaw (45 calories, page 110).*

Milano Chicken

1 T. vegetable oil

4 (4 to 4.5 oz. each) boneless, skinless chicken breast halves, trimmed of fat

2 cloves garlic, crushed

1 tsp. Italian seasoning

1 tsp. crushed red pepper flakes

Salt and pepper to taste

1 (28 oz.) can stewed tomatoes, drained

1 (9 oz.) pkg. frozen green beans

Heat the oil in a large skillet over medium-high heat. Season both sides of each chicken breast half with the garlic, Italian seasoning, red pepper flakes, salt and pepper. Place the chicken in the skillet and sauté for 5 minutes. Turn the chicken over and add the tomatoes to the skillet; cook for an additional 5 minutes. Add the green beans to the skillet and mix well. Cover the skillet, reduce the heat to medium-low and simmer for about 15 to 20 minutes, or until the chicken is cooked through.

Serving size: *1 chicken breast half plus ¼ of the vegetables (about ¾ cup)*
Calories: *241*
Fat: *5.3 g*

Suggested sides: *Balsamic Mandarin Salad (74 calories, page 101) or Spiced Brown Rice with Corn (133 calories, page 117).*

Lemon
Chipotle Chicken

Makes 4 servings

1 canned chipotle pepper in adobo sauce, minced

½ C. reduced-fat mayonnaise

Juice of 1 lemon

4 (4 to 4.5 oz. each) boneless, skinless chicken breast halves, trimmed of fat

¼ C. dry bread crumbs

In a small bowl, combine the minced pepper, mayonnaise and lemon juice. Arrange the chicken in an even layer in a baking dish. Brush a generous amount of the chipotle mixture over each chicken breast half; cover and refrigerate for 1 hour. Preheat the oven to 375°. Before baking, sprinkle 1 tablespoon bread crumbs over each chicken breast half. Bake for approximately 20 minutes or until the chicken is cooked through.

Serving size: *1 chicken breast half*
Calories: *208*
Fat: *8.1 g*

Suggested sides: *Stuffed Zucchini Boats (107 calories, page 105) or Scalloped Corn & Broccoli (162 calories, page 111).*

Feel the Burn!

Thirty minutes of swimming laps is not only refreshing, but you can burn more than 300 calories!

Apricot Honey Mustard Chicken

Makes 4 servings

4 (4 to 4.5 oz. each) boneless, skinless chicken breast halves, trimmed of fat

⅓ C. Dijon or honey mustard

3 T. apricot preserves

1 tsp. ground ginger

Preheat an outdoor grill to medium-high heat and lightly oil the grate. In a small bowl, whisk together mustard, apricot preserves and ginger. Set aside half of the mixture in a separate bowl. Brush the remaining mixture over the chicken. Grill the chicken for 6 to 8 minutes on each side, or until the chicken is cooked through, brushing with the reserved mustard mixture.

Serving size: *1 chicken breast half*
Calories: *201*
Fat: *3.1 g*

Suggested sides: *Corn Bread Custard (168 calories, page 120) or mashed garlic cauliflower (23 calories per serving, see page 44).*

Tropical Chicken Kabobs

Makes 4 servings

12 (10") wooden skewers

1½ T. low-sodium soy sauce

1½ T. brown sugar

1 T. sherry wine

1½ tsp. sesame oil

¼ tsp. ground ginger

Pinch of garlic powder

4 (4 to 4.5 oz. each) boneless, skinless chicken breast halves, trimmed of fat and cut into 2" cubes

1 (20 oz.) can pineapple chunks, drained

Soak the skewers in a large bowl of water; set aside. In a shallow dish, combine the soy sauce, brown sugar, sherry wine, sesame oil, ginger and garlic powder. Add the cubed chicken and pineapple to the dish, stirring until well coated. Cover the dish and refrigerate at least 2 hours to marinate. Preheat an outdoor grill to medium-high heat and lightly oil the grate. Thread the chicken and pineapple alternately onto the skewers. Grill for 15 to 20 minutes, turning occasionally, until the chicken is cooked through.

Serving size: *3 skewers of chicken and pineapple*
Calories: *203*
Fat: *4.2 g*

Suggested sides: *½ cup cooked white rice (103 calories), ½ cup cooked brown rice (108 calories) or ½ cup cooked wild rice (83 calories).*

Chicken in Balsamic Pear Sauce

Makes 6 servings

6 (4 to 4.5 oz. each) boneless, skinless chicken breast halves, trimmed of fat

Salt and pepper to taste

1 T. extra-virgin olive oil

1 shallot, chopped

2 medium pears, peeled, cored and sliced

1 C. low-sodium chicken broth

¼ C. balsamic vinegar

2 T. sugar

2 tsp. cornstarch

¼ C. dried tart cherries

Place the chicken breast halves between two sheets of plastic wrap. Using a meat mallet, carefully pound the chicken to about ½" thickness. Season both sides of each chicken breast half with salt and pepper. Heat the oil in a large skillet over medium-high heat. When the oil is hot, add the chicken to the skillet; sauté for 3 to 4 minutes on each side, or until golden brown. Transfer the chicken to a plate and keep warm. Add the shallot to the same skillet over medium-high heat; sauté for 2 minutes. Decrease the heat to medium and stir in the pears; sauté for 3 to 4 minutes, or until the pears are golden brown. In a small bowl, combine the chicken broth, balsamic vinegar, sugar and cornstarch; pour over the pears in the skillet. Stir in the cherries and increase the heat to high; simmer for 6 to 8 minutes or until the sauce thickens. Return the chicken to the skillet and decrease the heat to medium. Cook for 10 minutes, or until the chicken is cooked through.

Serving size: *1 chicken breast half plus ¼ of the fruit and sauce (about ½ cup)*
Calories: *233*
Fat: *4.1 g*

Suggested sides: *Mashed Turnip & Potatoes (100 calories, page 108) or Whole-Wheat Dinner Roll (132 calories, page 119).*

Couscous & Cranberry Turkey Burgers

Makes 6 servings

¼ C. plus 2 T. whole-wheat couscous
2 T. extra-virgin olive oil
1 small onion, finely chopped
1 stalk celery, minced
1 T. chopped fresh thyme

1½ tsp. chopped fresh sage
½ tsp. salt
½ tsp. pepper
¼ C. dried cranberries, finely chopped
1 lb. 93% lean ground turkey

Place the couscous in a large bowl. Pour ½ cup boiling water over the couscous; stir and set aside until the water is absorbed, about 5 minutes. Preheat an outdoor grill to medium-high heat and lightly oil the grate. Meanwhile, heat the olive oil in a large skillet over medium heat. Stir in the onion; sauté for 1 minute. Stir in the celery; sauté for about 3 minutes. Add the thyme, sage, salt and pepper; cook and stir for about 20 seconds. Transfer the onion mixture to the bowl with the couscous; stir in the cranberries until combined. Set aside the couscous to cool for about 5 minutes. Mix the ground turkey into the couscous mixture until combined, being careful not to over-mix. Shape the mixture into 6 patties. Grill the patties for 5 to 6 minutes, or until cooked through, turning carefully to avoid breaking.

If preparing on the stovetop, cook the patties in a large cast-iron skillet sprayed with non-stick cooking spray for 2 minutes. Carefully turn the patties over, reduce the heat to medium and cook for 4 minutes. Turn again to the first side and cook for another 2 minutes. Cover the skillet and continue to heat until the burgers are browned and cooked through.

Serving size: *1 turkey burger*
Calories: *217*
Fat: *10 g*

Suggested sides: *Spiced Grape Salad (70 calories, page 103) or Seasoned Green Beans & Cherry Tomatoes (122 calories, page 112). These burgers would taste great served between large crispy lettuce leaves (add just 5 calories for each large piece of iceberg lettuce). Otherwise, see page 45 for tips on choosing buns!*

Turkey Dill Burgers

Makes 6 servings

2 slices whole-wheat sandwich bread, crusts removed,
   torn into pieces
1 (8 oz.) pkg. white mushrooms
1 T. extra-virgin olive oil, divided
1 medium onion, finely chopped
2 cloves garlic, minced
1 lb. 93% lean ground turkey
1 large egg, lightly beaten
3 T. chopped fresh dill
1½ T. Dijon mustard
½ tsp. salt
¼ tsp. pepper

Pulse the bread pieces in a food processor until fine crumbs form. Transfer the bread crumbs to a large bowl. Pulse the mushrooms in the processor until finely chopped. Heat 2 teaspoons oil in a large non-stick skillet over medium-high heat. Stir the onion, garlic and chopped mushrooms into the skillet; sauté until tender and the liquid has evaporated, about 10 minutes. Remove from heat and stir in the bread crumbs; let cool for 15 to 20 minutes. Preheat an outdoor grill to medium-high heat and lightly oil the grate. Stir the turkey, egg, dill, mustard, salt and pepper into the mushroom mixture, mixing by hand until well combined. Form the mixture into 6 (½" thick) patties. Brush the patties with the remaining 1 teaspoon oil. Grill the patties for about 5 minutes per side, or until cooked through.

Serving size: *1 turkey burger*
Calories: *193*
Fat: *10 g*

Suggested sides: *Low-Fat Potato Salad (206 calories, page 104) or Cheesy & Easy Twice-Baked Potatoes (169 calories, page 118). See page 45 for tips on choosing buns!*

Mini Turkey Mushroom Loaves

Makes 6 servings

1 T. extra-virgin olive oil
⅔ C. finely diced celery
⅓ C. finely diced onion
1 (12 oz.) pkg. cremini mushrooms, finely chopped
⅓ oz. (½ C.) dried porcini mushrooms
1 large egg, lightly beaten
1½ lb. 93% lean ground turkey
⅓ C. whole-wheat bread crumbs
2 T. tomato paste
1 T. Worcestershire sauce
2 tsp. chopped fresh thyme
½ tsp. salt
½ tsp. pepper

Preheat the oven to 375°. Coat a large rimmed baking sheet with non-stick cooking spray; set aside. Heat the olive oil in a large skillet over medium heat. Add the celery and onion to the skillet; sauté for 2 to 3 minutes, or until softened. Stir in the cremini mushrooms; sauté for about 5 minutes. Transfer the sautéed mixture to a large bowl and set aside to cool for 10 minutes. Grind the dried mushrooms in a food processor until a powder forms. Stir the mushroom powder, egg, turkey, bread crumbs, tomato paste, Worcestershire sauce, thyme, salt and pepper into the sautéed mixture. Mix by hand until well combined. Divide the mixture into 6 portions, about ¾ cup each. Shape each portion into an oval loaf, about 4″ long and 2½″ wide. Place the loaves on the prepared baking sheet. Bake the loaves until lightly browned and cooked through, about 35 to 40 minutes.

Serving size: *1 mini turkey loaf*
Calories: *231*
Fat: *10 g*

Suggested sides: *Seasoned Green Beans & Cherry Tomatoes (122 calories, page 112) or Dilled Carrots (72 calories, page 114).*

Seafood

Easy Lemon Garlic Tilapia

Makes 4 servings

4 (3 oz.) tilapia fillets
3 T. fresh lemon juice
1 T. butter, melted
1 clove garlic, minced
1 tsp. dried parsley flakes
Pepper to taste

Preheat the oven to 375°. Spray a 9 x 13" baking dish with non-stick cooking spray. Rinse the fillets under cool water and pat dry with paper towels. Place the fillets in an even layer in the baking dish. Drizzle the lemon juice and butter over the fish. Sprinkle with the garlic, parsley and pepper; bake for about 30 minutes, or until the fish flakes easily with a fork.

Serving size: *1 fillet*
Calories: *142*
Fat: *4.4 g*

Suggested sides: *Lemony Green Beans (68 calories, page 100) or White Wine Herbed Mushrooms (55 calories, page 115).*

Sweet Ginger Perch

Makes 4 servings

12 oz. fresh or frozen ocean perch, red snapper or grouper fillets
⅛ tsp. pepper
1 C. low-sodium chicken broth
¼ C. sliced green onions
⅓ C. orange juice
2 T. reduced-sodium soy sauce
1 T. honey
1 tsp. toasted sesame oil
½ tsp. grated fresh gingerroot or ¼ tsp. ground ginger
6 C. torn mixed greens

Thaw the fish, if frozen. Rinse the fillets under cool water and pat dry with paper towels. Sprinkle both sides of fillets lightly with pepper; set aside. In a large skillet over medium-high heat, combine the chicken broth and green onions; bring to a boil. Add the fillets to the boiling broth and reduce the heat to a simmer. Cook, covered, for 4 to 6 minutes or until the fish flakes easily with a fork. Remove the fish to a plate and keep warm. Discard the cooking liquid. In the same skillet over medium-high heat, combine the orange juice, soy sauce, honey, sesame oil and ginger; bring to a boil. Boil, uncovered, for 1 minute, stirring once. Place the greens in a large bowl. Pour half of the ginger sauce over the greens; toss gently. Place ¼ of the greens on each of 4 serving plates; top each with an even portion of the cooked fish. Drizzle the remaining sauce over each serving.

Serving size: *1½ cups greens plus 3 ounces fish and 1 tablespoon sauce*
Calories: *177*
Fat: *3.2 g*

Suggested sides: *Whole-Wheat Dinner Rolls (132 calories, page 119) or Corn Bread Custard (168 calories, page 120).*

Cilantro Lime Fillets

Makes 4 servings

4 (4 oz.) cod or flounder fillets
¼ tsp. pepper
1½ tsp. extra-virgin olive oil
1½ tsp. dried onion flakes
1 clove garlic, minced
¾ tsp. ground cumin
2 T. minced fresh cilantro
1 lime, peeled and thinly sliced
1 T. margarine, melted

Preheat the oven to 375°. Place each fillet on a piece of heavy-duty foil. Sprinkle the fish with pepper. Heat the oil in a small saucepan over medium heat. Add the onion flakes and garlic; sauté for 1 minute. Stir in the cumin. Spoon the sautéed mixture over the fillets. Sprinkle ¼ of the cilantro over each fillet. Place a few lime slices over each fillet and drizzle with the margarine. Fold the foil over the fillets, sealing the edges. Place the foil packets on a baking sheet. Bake for 35 to 40 minutes, or until the fish flakes easily with a fork. Be careful to avoid the escaping steam when opening the packets.

Serving size: *1 fillet*
Calories: *143*
Fat: *5.4 g*

Suggested sides: *Rosemary Roasted Potatoes (227 calories, page 107) or Black Beans & Rice (135 calories, page 116).*

Teriyaki Grilled Salmon

Makes 4 servings

¼ C. low-sodium soy sauce
¼ C. dry sherry
1 T. rice wine vinegar
1 T. brown sugar
1 tsp. garlic powder
⅛ tsp. ground ginger
½ tsp. pepper
1 (16 oz.) skinless salmon fillet (1" thick)

In a shallow dish, combine the soy sauce, sherry, vinegar, brown sugar, garlic powder, ground ginger and pepper; stir well. Add the salmon to the dish, turning to coat in the marinade, and chill in the refrigerator for about 30 minutes. Preheat an outdoor grill to medium heat and lightly oil the grate. Carefully place the salmon on the hot grill, reserving the marinade. Grill the salmon for 5 to 7 minutes on each side, or until the salmon flakes easily with a fork. Transfer the fish to a serving platter and keep warm. Meanwhile, pour the reserved marinade in a small saucepan over medium-high heat. Bring to a boil for 5 minutes or until the marinade becomes thick and syrupy. Divide the fillet into 4 portions. Place one portion on each of 4 serving plates; spoon ¼ of the sauce over each portion. Serve immediately.

Serving size: 4 ounces salmon plus about 1 tablespoon sauce
Calories: 219
Fat: 4 g

Suggested sides: Lemony Green Beans (68 calories, page 100) or Dilled Carrots (72 calories, page 114).

Fenneled Fish

12 oz. fresh or frozen ocean perch, red snapper or
   grouper fillets
Salt and pepper to taste
1 fennel bulb, sliced
1 large onion, chopped
2 medium carrots, chopped
2 cloves garlic, minced
1 T. extra-virgin olive oil
¼ C. low-sodium chicken broth
2 T. snipped fresh dill or 1½ tsp. dried dillweed
¼ tsp. salt
¼ tsp. pepper

Thaw the fish, if frozen. Preheat the oven to 450°. Rinse the fillets under cool water and pat dry with paper towels. Sprinkle both sides of fillets lightly with salt and pepper; set aside. In a large skillet over medium heat, sauté the fennel, onion, carrots and garlic in olive oil until the vegetables are tender, about 7 to 9 minutes. Remove the skillet from heat and stir in the chicken broth, dill, ¼ teaspoon salt and ¼ teaspoon pepper. Transfer ¾ of the sautéed vegetables to a 2-quart baking dish. Place the fish fillets over the vegetables, tucking under any thin edges. Spoon the remaining vegetables and liquid over the fish. Bake, uncovered, for about 12 minutes, or until the fish flakes easily with a fork.

Serving size: *3 ounces fish plus ¼ of the vegetables (about 1 cup)*
Calories: *198*
Fat: *5.6 g*

Suggested sides: *Spiced Grape Salad (70 calories, page 103) or Mashed Turnip & Potatoes (100 calories, page 108).*

Orange Roughy with Simple Garden Salsa

Makes 4 servings

1 medium tomato, finely chopped
2 T. vegetable oil
1 tsp. steak seasoning
½ tsp. dried thyme
4 (4 oz.) orange roughy fillets

Preheat an outdoor grill to medium-high heat and cover the grate with aluminum foil coated with non-stick cooking spray, greased side up. In a medium bowl, toss together the tomato, oil, steak seasoning and thyme. Place the fish fillets on the foil over the preheated grill. Divide the tomato mixture evenly over the fillets. Cook the fillets for 10 minutes, or until the fish flakes easily with a fork. Do not turn the fillets over during grilling.

Serving size: *4 ounces fish plus ¼ of the salsa (about ½ cup)*
Calories: *147*
Fat: *7.7 g*

Suggested sides: *Quinoa with Black Beans (154 calories, page 106) or Tasty Breaded Brussels (75 calories, page 109).*

Basil & Parmesan-
Encrusted Tilapia

Makes 4 servings

2 lbs. skinless tilapia fillets
Pepper to taste
2 T. dried basil
½ C. grated Parmesan cheese
4 tsp. extra-virgin olive oil

Preheat the oven broiler to high heat. Cut the tilapia fillets lengthwise into two pieces. Rinse the fillets under cool water and pat dry with paper towels. Sprinkle both sides of the fillets lightly with pepper. In a small bowl, combine the basil and Parmesan cheese; set aside. Heat the oil in a large oven-safe skillet over medium-high heat. Sauté the fish pieces for 3 minutes on one side, or until lightly browned. Remove the skillet from the heat and turn the fish pieces over. Sprinkle the Parmesan mixture over the fish. Place the skillet under the broiler and cook until the fish flakes easily with a fork and the cheese is lightly browned, about 3 to 4 minutes.

Serving size: *8 ounces fish (about 4 pieces)*
Calories: *314*
Fat: *10.3 g*

Suggested sides: *Lemony Green Beans (68 calories, page 100) or Broccoli Garden Toss (45.5 calories, page 102).*

Spicy Szechwan Shrimp

2 T. ketchup
1 T. low-sodium soy sauce
2 tsp. cornstarch
1 tsp. honey
½ tsp. crushed red pepper
¼ tsp. ground ginger
1 T. vegetable oil
¼ C. sliced green onions
4 cloves garlic, minced
2 lbs. cooked shrimp, peels and tails removed

In a medium bowl, combine 4 tablespoons water, ketchup, soy sauce, cornstarch, honey, crushed red pepper and ground ginger; set aside. Heat the oil in a large skillet over medium-high heat. Stir in the green onions and garlic; sauté for 30 seconds. Add the shrimp and toss to coat with oil. Stir in the sauce. Continue to cook until the shrimp are heated and the sauce is bubbly and thick.

Serving size: *¼ of recipe (8 ounces shrimp coated in sauce)*
Calories: *282*
Fat: *5.9 g*

Suggested side: *½ cup cooked wild rice (83 calories).*

Sweet Horseradish-
Glazed Salmon

⅓ C. apple jelly

1 T. minced fresh chives

2 T. prepared horseradish

1 T. champagne or white wine vinegar

½ tsp. salt, divided

4 (6 oz.) skinless salmon fillets (1" thick)

¼ tsp. pepper

2 tsp. extra-virgin olive oil

Preheat the oven to 350°. In a medium bowl, combine the apple jelly, chives, horseradish, vinegar and ¼ teaspoon salt; whisk until well mixed. Sprinkle the salmon fillets with the pepper and remaining ¼ teaspoon salt. Heat the oil in a large oven-safe skillet over medium heat. Add the salmon and cook for 3 minutes on one side. Turn the salmon over and brush with half of the glaze mixture. Bake the salmon for 5 minutes or until the fish flakes easily with a fork. Brush the remaining glaze mixture over the salmon and serve immediately.

Serving size: *¼ of recipe (1 fillet)*
Calories: *375*
Fat: *16.8 g*

Suggested side: *10 steamed sugar snap peas (14 calories).*

Lighter Fish Sticks

Makes 4 serving

1 C. whole-wheat dry
   bread crumbs
1 C. whole-grain
   flake cereal
1 tsp. lemon pepper
½ tsp. garlic powder
½ tsp. paprika

¼ tsp. salt
½ C. flour
2 large egg whites,
   beaten
1 lb. tilapia fillets, cut into
   ½" x 3" strips

Preheat the oven to 450°. Set a wire rack on a baking sheet; coat with non-stick cooking spray. In a food processor or blender, combine the bread crumbs, cereal, lemon pepper, garlic powder, paprika and salt; process until finely ground. Transfer the coating to a shallow dish. Place the flour in a separate shallow dish and the egg whites in a third shallow dish. Dredge each fish piece first in the flour, then in the egg white. Finally, coat both sides of each fish piece in the bread crumb mixture. Spray both sides of the breaded fish lightly with non-stick cooking spray. Place the fish on the prepared rack. Bake until the fish is cooked through and the breading is golden brown and crisp, about 10 minutes.

Serving size: *about 4 or 5 fish sticks*
Calories: *274*
Fat: *3 g*

Suggested sides: *Guilt-Free Zesty Coleslaw (45 calories, page 110) with Fat-Free Tartar Sauce on the side (recipe below).*

Fat-Free Tartar Sauce!

For just 16.5 calories and 0 grams of fat per serving, whip up your own tartar sauce by mixing ¼ cup fat-free mayonnaise, 1 tablespoon sweet pickle relish, 1 chopped green onion and ¾ teaspoon red wine vinegar. Divide into four portions.

Pan-Seared Trout & Spinach

Makes 4 servings

2 C. fish broth or low-sodium chicken broth

2 T. light whipping cream

Pinch of saffron

2 tsp. fresh lemon juice

Salt and pepper to taste

1 tsp. extra-virgin olive oil, divided

4 (5 oz.) trout fillets

1 lb. fresh spinach leaves, rinsed and dried

1 lemon, quartered

Combine the fish broth and cream in a small saucepan over high heat; boil until the liquid has reduced to ⅓ cup, about 25 minutes. Remove the liquid from the heat; add the saffron threads and let steep for 10 minutes. Stir in the lemon juice and season with salt and pepper to taste. Heat ½ teaspoon oil in a large skillet over medium-high heat. Sprinkle both sides of each trout fillet with salt and pepper. Sauté two fillets in the pan until crispy and golden brown on one side, about 5 minutes. Remove the pan from the heat and turn the fillets over; let rest in the hot skillet until cooked through, about 2 minutes. Remove the fillets to a plate and keep warm. Add the remaining ½ teaspoon oil to the skillet and repeat with the remaining two fillets. After they are cooked, remove the fillets to the same plate and keep warm. Add the spinach to the pan and cook until it wilts, about 2 to 3 minutes. Divide the wilted spinach into 4 portions and place one portion on each of 4 serving plates. Place one trout fillet next to the spinach on each plate. Spoon ¼ of the saffron sauce over the spinach and fish on each plate. Garnish each serving with a lemon wedge.

Serving size: 1 fillet plus ¼ of the spinach mixture (about 1 cup spinach and 1½ tablespoons sauce)
Calories: 252
Fat: 12 g

Suggested sides: Mashed Turnip & Potatoes (100 calories, page 108) or Quick Garlic Asparagus (106 calories, page 113).

Corn & Cilantro Crab Cakes

Makes 4 servings

5 tsp. canola oil, divided
1 C. fresh or frozen corn kernels
¼ C. finely chopped onion
½ tsp. curry powder
1 clove garlic, minced
1 lb. lump crabmeat, picked over

⅓ C. reduced-fat mayonnaise
2 large egg whites
2 T. lime juice
3 T. chopped fresh cilantro
2 T. chopped fresh mint
¼ tsp. salt
1 C. dry bread crumbs, divided

Preheat the oven to 450°. Coat a baking sheet with non-stick cooking spray; set aside. Heat 1 teaspoon oil in a large non-stick skillet over medium-high heat. Add corn, onion, curry powder and garlic; sauté until vegetables are soft, about 5 minutes. Transfer sautéed mixture to a large bowl and let cool for 10 minutes. Flake crabmeat and stir into bowl. In a small bowl, whisk together mayonnaise, egg whites, lime juice, cilantro, mint and salt; fold into crab mixture along with ½ cup bread crumbs. Using about ⅓ cup per patty, form mixture into eight ¾"-thick patties. Dredge patties in remaining ½ cup bread crumbs. Heat 2 teaspoons oil in a large non-stick skillet over medium heat. Add four crab cakes to skillet and cook for 2 to 3 minutes, or until golden on one side. Turn crab cakes over onto prepared baking sheet. Add remaining 2 teaspoons oil to skillet and cook remaining four crab cakes; transfer to baking sheet. Bake crab cakes until golden on the second side and heated through, about 15 to 20 minutes.

Serving size: 2 crab cakes
Calories: 343
Fat: 14 g
Suggested sides: mashed garlic cauliflower (23 calories per serving, see page 44) and Crab Cake Sauce (recipe below).

Crab Cake Sauce

To make your own Crab Cake Sauce, combine ¼ cup ketchup, ¼ cup chopped fresh parsley, 1 tablespoon horseradish, 2 teaspoons white vinegar, 1 teaspoon grated lemon peel and 1 teaspoon hot sauce; mix well. Divide into four portions. Each 1½ tablespoon serving is just 18 calories and fat-free!

Cheesy Shrimp & Grits Casserole

Makes 6 servings

2 C. reduced-fat 2% milk
¾ C. low-sodium chicken broth
1 C. uncooked quick-cooking grits
¼ tsp. salt
½ C. shredded Parmesan cheese
2 T. butter
1 (3 oz.) pkg. reduced-fat cream cheese
3 T. chopped fresh parsley
1 T. chopped fresh chives
1 T. fresh lemon juice
2 large egg whites
1 lb. cooked shrimp, peels and tails removed,
   coarsely chopped
Hot sauce, optional

Preheat the oven to 375°. In a medium saucepan over medium heat, combine the milk and broth; bring to a boil. Gradually stir the grits and salt into the pan, stirring constantly with a whisk. Cook for 5 minutes or until thick, stirring constantly. Remove the saucepan from the heat. Stir in the Parmesan cheese, butter and cream cheese. Fold in the parsley, chives, lemon juice, egg whites and chopped shrimp. Spoon the mixture into a 7 x 11" baking dish sprayed with non-stick cooking spray. Bake for 25 minutes, or until set. If desired, serve with hot sauce on the side.

Serving size: ⅙ *of recipe (about 1 cup)*
Calories: 341
Fat: 13 g

Suggested sides: 5 steamed broccoli flowerets (about 60 calories) or 10 steamed asparagus spears (about 30 calories).

Scallop Tacos

Makes 4 servings

1 lb. sea scallops

Fresh lemon or lime juice

Seasoning salt

2 C. shredded cabbage

4 to 6 green onions, thinly sliced

½ C. chopped fresh cilantro

¼ C. reduced-fat mayonnaise

2 T. cider vinegar

Pinch of Splenda

Dash of hot sauce

Salt and pepper to taste

4 (6") reduced-fat flour, corn or wheat tortillas, warmed

Wash the scallops gently under cool water and pat dry with paper towels. Place the scallops in a large resealable plastic bag. Sprinkle some lemon or lime juice and seasoning salt over the scallops; toss until coated. Seal the bag and refrigerate for 30 minutes to 1 hour. In a medium bowl, combine the cabbage, green onions, cilantro, mayonnaise, vinegar, Splenda, hot sauce, salt and pepper; cover and refrigerate. Remove scallops from the bag, drain well and pat dry with paper towels. Heat a large non-stick skillet over medium-high heat and spray it lightly with oil or non-stick cooking spray. Add the scallops and sear for 2 to 3 minutes on each side or until golden brown and cooked through, being careful not to overcook. Divide the scallops into four portions. Place ¼ of the cabbage mixture on each tortilla and top each with one portion of the scallops. Fold up sides and serve immediately.

Serving size: *1 taco*
Calories: *251*
Fat: *3.3 g*

Suggested sides: *Black Beans & Rice (135 calories, page 116) or Spiced Brown Rice with Corn (133 calories, page 117).*

Crab Quesadillas

Makes 4 servings

1 C. shredded reduced-fat Cheddar cheese

2 oz. reduced-fat cream cheese

4 scallions, chopped

½ medium red bell pepper, seeded and finely chopped

⅓ C. chopped fresh cilantro

2 T. chopped jalapenos, optional

1 tsp. grated orange zest

1 T. orange juice

½ lb. lump crabmeat, picked over

4 (8") whole-wheat tortillas

2 tsp. canola oil, divided

In a medium bowl, combine the Cheddar cheese, cream cheese, scallions, bell pepper, cilantro, jalapenos, orange zest and orange juice; mix well. Flake the crabmeat and gently fold into the cheese mixture. Spread ¼ of the filling over half of each tortilla. Fold the tortillas in half over the filling, pressing gently. Heat 1 teaspoon oil in a large non-stick skillet over medium heat. Place 2 quesadillas in the pan and cook, turning once, until golden on both sides, about 3 to 4 minutes total. Transfer the quesadilla to a cutting board and keep warm. Add the remaining 1 teaspoon oil to the skillet and cook the remaining 2 quesadillas. Cut each quesadilla into 4 wedges and serve immediately.

Serving size: *1 quesadilla (4 wedges)*
Calories: *303*
Fat: *11 g*

Suggested sides: *Baked Tortilla Chips (56 calories per serving, see page 86) or ¼ cup of canned heated black beans or pinto beans (60 calories).*

Simply Citrus
Orange Roughy

Makes 4 servings

1 T. extra-virgin olive oil
4 (4 oz.) orange roughy fillets
Juice of 1 orange
Juice of 1 lemon
½ tsp. lemon pepper seasoning

Heat the oil in a large skillet over medium-high heat. Arrange the fillet in the skillet. Drizzle the orange and lemon juice over the fish; sprinkle with the lemon pepper seasoning. Cook for 5 minutes, or until the fish flakes easily with a fork.

Serving size: *1 fillet*
Calories: *133*
Fat: *4.3 g*

Suggested sides: *Broccoli Garden Toss (45.5 calories, page 102), Stuffed Zucchini Boats (107 calories, page 105) or Scalloped Corn & Broccoli (162 calories, page 111).*

Feel the Burn!

Go fish! An hour of moderate-paced fishing (including casting and reeling) will burn about 300 calories.

Trout with Lentil-Veggie Toss

Makes 4 servings

1 tsp. extra-virgin olive oil

¼ C. chopped leek

¼ C. finely chopped carrot

2 cloves garlic, minced

1 C. dried lentils

1 (14 oz.) can low-sodium chicken broth

¼ C. chopped celery

1 T. finely chopped parsley

1 T. sherry vinegar

¾ tsp. salt, divided

½ tsp. pepper, divided

2 (6 oz.) trout fillets

Heat the oil in a medium saucepan over medium-high heat. Stir in the leek, carrot and garlic; sauté for 2 minutes. Next, stir in the lentils, chicken broth and ½ cup water; bring to a boil. Cover the saucepan and reduce the heat to medium-low; simmer for 25 minutes or until the lentils are tender and the liquid is nearly absorbed. Remove the saucepan from the heat and stir in the celery, parsley, vinegar, ½ teaspoon salt and ¼ teaspoon pepper; stir until combined. Preheat the oven broiler to high heat. Sprinkle both sides of each trout fillet with the remaining salt and pepper. Place the fish on a baking sheet sprayed with non-stick cooking spray. Broil the fish for 5 minutes, or until it flakes easily with a fork. Break the fish into chunks and toss gently with the lentil mixture. Divide the mixture into 4 portions and place one portion on each of 4 serving plates.

Serving size: *3 ounces fish plus ¼ of the vegetables (about 1 cup lentil and veggie mix)*
Calories: *311*
Fat: *6.2 g*
Suggested sides: *10 grapes (34 calories) or 2 small cantaloupe wedges (38 calories).*

Soup &
Other Stuff

Out-of-the-Can
Tortilla Soup

Makes 6 servings

1 (15 oz.) can whole kernel corn, drained

2 (14.5 oz.) cans low-sodium chicken broth

1 (10 oz.) can chunk chicken, drained

1 (15 oz.) can black beans, undrained

1 (10 oz.) can diced tomatoes with green chilies, drained

In a large pot over medium heat, pour the corn, chicken broth, chicken, black beans with liquid, and tomatoes; mix until combined. Bring the soup to a simmer until the chicken is heated through.

Serving size: *⅙ of recipe (about 1 cup)*
Calories: *222*
Fat: *5.8 g*

Suggested side: *Baked Tortilla Chips (recipe below)*

Get Baked!

Bake up some delicious tortilla chips to serve with this soup. Cut 6 corn tortillas into 8 wedges. Dip the wedges in water and spread on a baking sheet. Sprinkle with a little chili powder and bake at 450° until crisp, about 5 to 8 minutes. A serving of 8 chips is only 56 calories and 1 gram of fat.

Loaded with Veggies Minestrone

Makes 8 servings

3 T. extra-virgin olive oil

3 cloves garlic, minced

2 onions, chopped

2 C. chopped celery

5 carrots, sliced

2 C. low-sodium chicken broth

4 C. tomato sauce

1 C. canned kidney beans, rinsed and drained

1 (15 oz.) can green beans, drained

2 C. baby spinach, rinsed

3 zucchinis, quartered and sliced

1 T. chopped fresh oregano

2 T. chopped fresh basil

Salt and pepper to taste

½ C. uncooked small shell pasta

2 T. grated Parmesan cheese

Heat the oil in a large soup pot over medium-low heat. Add the garlic; sauté for 2 to 3 minutes. Stir in the onion; sauté for 4 to 5 minutes. Add the celery and carrots; sauté for 1 to 2 minutes. Stir in the chicken broth, tomato sauce and 2 cups water; bring to a boil, stirring often. Reduce the heat to low and add the kidney beans, green beans, spinach, zucchini, oregano, basil, salt and pepper. Simmer for 30 to 40 minutes. Meanwhile, cook the pasta in a pot of lightly salted, boiling water until al dente, about 8 to 10 minutes. Drain the pasta and set aside. To serve, place 2 tablespoons cooked pasta in each of 8 serving bowls. Ladle the soup over the pasta into the bowls. Sprinkle a little Parmesan cheese over each serving; serve immediately.

Serving size: *⅛ of recipe (about 1½ cups)*
Calories: *232*
Fat: *8.3 g*

Suggested side: *Whole-Wheat Dinner Rolls (132 calories, page 119).*

Black Bean Soup

Makes 4 servings

1 onion, finely chopped
2 cloves garlic, minced
2 stalks celery, finely chopped
¼ large red bell pepper, seeded and finely chopped
2 chicken bouillon cubes
2 (15 oz.) cans black beans, undrained
½ tsp. salt
½ tsp. ground cumin
1½ T. cornstarch
Juice of ½ lemon

In a large pot over medium heat, combine the onion, garlic, celery, bell pepper, bouillon cubes and 1½ cups boiling water; simmer for 10 minutes. Stir in half a can of beans, salt and cumin. Puree the soup in a blender and return it to the pot, or use an immersion blender right in the pot. Stir in the remaining black beans. In a small bowl, combine the cornstarch and 1½ tablespoons water. Stir the cornstarch mixture and lemon juice into the soup; continue to heat until thickened.

Serving size: *¼ of recipe (about 1 cup)*
Calories: *207*
Fat: *0.8 g*

Suggested side: *Corn Bread Custard (168 calories, page 120).*

Creamy Tomato Soup

½ C. butter

2 T. extra-virgin olive oil

1 large onion, thinly sliced

1 tsp. thyme

1 tsp. basil

Salt and pepper to taste

2 (14.5 oz. cans) Italian-stewed tomatoes, drained

3 T. tomato paste

4 T. flour

3¾ C. low-sodium chicken broth, divided

1 tsp. sugar

1 C. heavy cream or half n' half

Heat the butter and oil in a large pot over medium-high heat. Stir in the onion, thyme, basil, salt and pepper; sauté for 3 to 4 minutes. Stir in the tomatoes and tomato paste. Reduce the heat to medium and simmer for 20 minutes. In a small bowl, whisk together the flour and 5 tablespoons chicken broth; stir into the soup. Add the remaining broth and simmer for 30 minutes, stirring occasionally. Puree the soup in a blender and return it to the pot, or use an immersion blender right in the pot. Stir in the sugar and cream; simmer for 5 minutes or until heated through.

Serving size: *⅛ of recipe (about 1 cup)*
Calories: *257*
Fat: *21.6 g*

Suggested sides: *Mix-ins for your soup! Add 15 Pepperidge Farm Original Goldfish crackers (41 calories), 2 tablespoons low-fat shredded Cheddar cheese (98 calories), 1 tablespoon light sour cream (20 calories), or ½ cup shredded cooked skinless chicken (124 calories).*

Garden Harvest Chicken Stew

Makes 10 servings

2 C. chopped onion
2 C. cooked and cubed boneless, skinless chicken breast
1 C. chopped celery
2 C. whole peeled tomatoes, undrained
2 C. sliced carrots
5 C. low-sodium chicken broth
1 C. fresh or frozen corn kernels
1 C. fresh or frozen peas
1 C. sliced zucchini

In a large pot over medium heat, combine the onion, chicken, celery, tomatoes with liquid, carrots, chicken broth, corn, peas and zucchini; mix well. Reduce the heat to medium-low and simmer for 30 minutes, or until the vegetables are tender and the chicken is heated through.

Serving size: *⅙ of recipe (about 1 cup)*
Calories: *211*
Fat: *5 g*

Suggested sides: *Want some crackers with your soup? Check the labels! Some little crackers can be packed with almost 40 calories apiece! Some better-for-you choices are Original Wheat Thins at 9 calories each, Regular Saltine crackers at about 13 calories each, Original Ritz butter crackers at 16 calories each, and Keebler Original Club crackers at 17.5 calories each.*

Tilapia Corn Chowder

1 tsp. canola oil
1 stalk celery, diced
1 leek, halved and thinly sliced
½ tsp. salt
½ tsp. pepper
4 C. low-sodium chicken broth
8 oz. Yukon Gold potatoes, diced
2 C. fresh or frozen corn kernels
1½ lbs. tilapia fillets, cut into bite-size pieces
1 tsp. finely chopped fresh thyme
1 C. half n' half
2 tsp. lemon juice
2 slices bacon, cooked crisp and crumbled
2 T. chopped fresh chives

Heat the oil in a large Dutch oven or pot over medium heat. Stir in the celery, leek, salt and pepper; sauté for 2 minutes. Stir in the chicken broth, potatoes and corn; bring to a low simmer. Continue to cook until the potatoes are just tender, about 8 minutes. Stir in the tilapia and thyme; return to a gentle simmer, heating until the tilapia is cooked through, about 4 minutes. Remove the pot from the heat and stir in the half n' half, lemon juice and crumbled bacon. Ladle the chowder into bowls; garnish each serving with some chopped chives.

Serving size: *⅙ of recipe (about 1¼ cups)*
Calories: *288*
Fat: *10 g*

Suggested sides: *Broccoli Garden Toss (45.5 calories, page 102) or 1 slice toasted wheat bread (about 65 calories).*

Artichoke Pizza
on Focaccia

Makes 8 servings

1 (14 oz.) can artichoke hearts, drained and quartered

1 red bell pepper, seeded and chopped

2 C. shredded Italian cheese blend

1 C. grated Parmesan cheese, divided

½ C. chopped fresh parsley

½ C. low-fat mayonnaise

2 cloves garlic, minced

1 tsp. pepper

¼ tsp. cayenne pepper

1 (10") focaccia bread loaf, cut horizontally

2 T. extra-virgin olive oil

Preheat the oven to 375°. In a medium bowl, combine the quartered artichokes, bell pepper, Italian cheese, ½ cup Parmesan cheese, parsley, mayonnaise, garlic, pepper and cayenne pepper; mix well. Place each focaccia half on a baking sheet; drizzle each with 1 tablespoon oil and sprinkle each with ¼ cup Parmesan cheese. Divide the artichoke mixture in half and spread one half on each focaccia loaf. Bake for 20 to 25 minutes, or until the cheese is bubbly and the toppings are hot. Remove the pizzas from the oven and let sit for 2 to 3 minutes. Cut each pizza into 8 slices.

Serving size: *2 pizza slices or ¼ of 1 pizza*
Calories: *368*
Fat: *25.7 g*

Suggested sides: *½ cup sliced strawberries (26 calories), 1 small peach (31 calories) or ½ cup diced watermelon (23 calories).*

Spinach Greek-Style Pizza

Makes 8 servings

1 lb. frozen bread dough, thawed
1 lb. ground skinless chicken
1 C. chopped onion
1 C. seeded and chopped red or green bell pepper
1 tsp. minced garlic
1 (15 oz.) can Italian-style tomato sauce
½ tsp. oregano
1 (10 oz.) pkg. frozen chopped spinach, thawed and drained
1 C. shredded reduced-fat part-skim mozzarella cheese
½ C. grated Parmesan cheese

Preheat the oven to 375°. Spray a 12" pizza pan with non-stick cooking spray. Press the dough into the pan, forming a 1" crust around the edge. Prick the dough with a fork. Bake the dough for 10 minutes. Meanwhile, in a medium skillet over medium-high heat, cook the ground chicken, onion, bell pepper and garlic until the chicken is cooked through and no longer pink. Stir in the tomato sauce and oregano; set aside. Remove the crust from the oven; sprinkle drained spinach over top. Spread the chicken sauce mixture over the spinach. Sprinkle the mozzarella and Parmesan cheese over the sauce. Bake for 25 minutes, or until the crust is lightly browned and the cheese is bubbly. Remove the pizza from the oven and let sit for 2 to 3 minutes; cut into 8 slices.

Serving size: *1 pizza slice*
Calories: *273*
Fat: *3 g*

Suggested sides: *Balsamic Mandarin Salad (74 calories, page 101) or Quick Garlic Asparagus (106 calories, page 113).*

Chicken
Cobb Salad

9 C. shredded romaine lettuce

2½ C. cooked and shredded boneless, skinless
   chicken breast

3 hard-boiled eggs, yolks removed, whites chopped

3 tomatoes, chopped

6 T. crumbled blue cheese

4 slices turkey bacon, cooked crisp and crumbled

1 avocado, peeled, pitted and diced

⅓ C. chopped green onions

¾ C. light ranch salad dressing

Divide the shredded lettuce into 6 individual bowls. Arrange an even portion of the chicken, chopped egg whites, tomatoes, blue cheese, crumbled bacon, avocado and green onions over the lettuce in each bowl. Drizzle about 2 tablespoons dressing over each salad.

Serving size: *⅙ of recipe (about 2 cups)*
Calories: *324*
Fat: *18 g*

Suggested side: *Crazy Fruit Kabobs (recipe below)*

Crazy Fruit Kabobs

*To make Crazy Fruit Kabobs, simply thread various fruits onto 10"
skewers. A kabob that contains 2 large strawberries, 2 cantaloupe
pieces, 2 large pineapple chunks and 3 large grapes is about
55 calories.*

Southwestern Beef Salad

3 T. vegetable oil
2 T. lime juice
2 T. low-sodium soy sauce
1¼ tsp. lemon pepper seasoning
1 tsp. garlic powder
1 lb. boneless sirloin steak, thinly sliced
6 C. assorted salad greens
1 red bell pepper, seeded and cut into strips
1 yellow bell pepper, seeded and cut into strips
2 green onions, chopped

In a large resealable plastic bag, combine the vegetable oil, lime juice, soy sauce, lemon pepper seasoning and garlic powder; mix to combine. Add the steak slices to the bag. Seal the bag and turn to coat the steak slices; chill in the refrigerator for 15 to 30 minutes to marinate. Arrange the salad greens into 4 individual bowls. Heat a large skillet over high heat. Cook the steak slices in the skillet for 2 to 3 minutes, or to desired doneness, discarding the marinade. Divide the steak slices into 4 portions; place one portion over the greens in each bowl. Top each with some of the bell pepper strips and green onions.

Serving size: *¼ of recipe (about 2 cups)*
Calories: *377*
Fat: *27.6 g*

Suggested side: *1 (0.3 oz.) package of sugar-free gelatin prepared with 8 large sliced strawberries (about 20 calories per 1-cup serving).*

Turkey Taco Salad

1 tsp. canola oil

1 large onion, chopped

4 cloves garlic, minced

1 lb. 93% lean ground turkey

2 Roma tomatoes, diced

1 (15 oz.) can kidney beans, drained and rinsed

2 tsp. ground cumin

2 tsp. chili powder

¼ tsp. salt

¼ C. chopped fresh cilantro

1 C. prepared salsa

¼ C. reduced-fat sour cream

8 C. shredded romaine lettuce

½ C. shredded sharp Cheddar cheese

Heat the oil in a large non-stick skillet over medium heat. Add the onion and garlic; sauté for 1 to 2 minutes. Stir in the turkey and heat until cooked through. Stir in the tomatoes, beans, cumin, chili powder and salt; cook, stirring occasionally, until the tomato softens, about 2 minutes. Remove the mixture from the heat and stir in the cilantro. In a small bowl, combine the salsa and sour cream. Stir ¼ cup of the salsa mixture into the skillet. Place the lettuce in a large salad bowl. Pour the remaining salsa mixture over the salad; toss until coated. Divide the salad into four portions; place one portion on each plate. Top each serving with an even portion of the turkey mixture. Sprinkle each serving with 2 tablespoons cheese. Serve immediately.

Serving size: ¼ of recipe (about 3 cups)
Calories: 343
Fat: 13 g

Suggested side: Crazy Fruit Kabobs (see page 94).

Roasted Shrimp Salad with Raspberries

1 lb. cooked shrimp, peels and tails removed

2 T. extra-virgin olive oil, divided

6 C. shredded romaine lettuce

2 C. fresh raspberries

2 C. fresh or canned pineapple chunks

2 medium tomatoes, cut into wedges

¼ C. pineapple juice

2 T. chopped fresh basil

1 T. balsamic vinegar

1 T. Dijon mustard

¼ tsp. salt

¼ tsp. pepper

Preheat an outdoor grill or oven broiler to medium-high heat. Toss the shrimp with 1 teaspoon oil in a medium bowl. Place the shrimp on the grill rack or a non-stick broiler pan about 4" from the heat. Grill or broil for 2 to 3 minutes on each side or until the shrimp turns opaque and is cooked through. Divide the lettuce, raspberries, pineapple chunks and tomato wedges evenly onto four plates. In a small jar, combine the pineapple juice, basil, vinegar, mustard, salt, pepper and remaining 5 teaspoons oil; cover with the lid and shake vigorously until well combined. Divide the cooked shrimp evenly onto the plates and drizzle an even amount of the dressing over each salad.

Serving size: *¼ of recipe (about 3 cups)*
Calories: *290*
Fat: *10 g*

Suggested side: *1 whole-wheat pita pocket (4" round) spread with 1 wedge of Laughing Cow light spreadable cheese (109 calories).*

Spicy Pork
Lettuce Wraps

Makes 4 servings

2 T. oyster sauce

1 T. hoisin sauce

1 T. rice vinegar

1 T. dry sherry

2 tsp. cornstarch

1 tsp. brown sugar

1 tsp. reduced-sodium
  soy sauce

1 tsp. sesame oil

1 T. canola oil, divided

1 lb. thin boneless pork
  chops, trimmed of fat
  and cut into thin strips

2 cloves garlic, minced

1 T. minced fresh ginger

1 (8 oz.) can sliced water
  chestnuts, drained
  and chopped

1 (8 oz.) can sliced
  bamboo shoots,
  drained and chopped

1 (8 oz.) pkg. shiitake
  mushrooms, cut into
  thin strips

12 large iceberg
  lettuce leaves

4 scallions, sliced

In a small bowl, combine the oyster sauce, hoisin sauce, vinegar, sherry, cornstarch, brown sugar, soy sauce and sesame oil; set aside. Heat 2 teaspoons canola oil in a wok or large non-stick skillet over medium-high heat. Add the pork, stirring constantly, until cooked through, about 4 minutes; transfer to a plate and keep warm. Wipe out the pan. Add the remaining 1 teaspoon canola oil, garlic and ginger to the wok or skillet; cook and stir for about 30 seconds. Stir in the water chestnuts, bamboo shoots and mushrooms; cook until softened, about 30 seconds. Return the pork to the pan and stir in the sauce. Cook until this sauce thickens, about 1 minute. Spoon about ⅓ cup of the filling into each lettuce leaf, sprinkle with scallions, roll up and serve.

Serving size: ¼ of recipe (3 lettuce wraps, or about 1 cup filling and 3 lettuce leaves)
Calories: 331
Fat: 16 g
Suggested side: Miso Soup is the perfect accompaniment for spicy lettuce wraps. In a medium saucepan over medium-high heat, combine 2 teaspoons dashi granules and 4 cups water; bring to a boil. Reduce the heat to medium and whisk in 3 tablespoons miso paste. Dice an 8-ounce package of silken tofu and stir into the soup along with 2 chopped green onions; simmer for about 3 minutes. Divide the soup into four bowls. Each serving is about 60 calories.

Pick-A-
Side Dish

Lemony Green Beans

4 C. fresh green beans, ends trimmed
¼ C. fresh lemon juice
2 tsp. grated lemon zest
Pepper to taste
1 T. extra-virgin olive oil

Fill a large pot halfway with water and bring to a boil over medium-high heat. Add the beans to the boiling water, then reduce the heat to medium. Cook the beans for 5 minutes, or until bright green and still crisp. Meanwhile, in a medium microwave-safe bowl, combine the lemon juice, lemon zest, pepper and oil. Drain the beans and run them under cold water. Shake off any excess water and add the beans to the lemon juice mixture; toss until evenly coated. Heat the green beans for about 30 seconds in the microwave, or until warm. Divide the green beans into 4 servings.

Serving size: *¼ of recipe (1 cup green beans)*
Calories: *68*
Fat: *3.5 g*

Balsamic Mandarin Salad

Makes 4 servings

4 C. mixed salad greens
1 kiwi fruit, peeled and sliced
½ (11 oz.) can mandarin oranges, drained
½ small red onion, chopped
1 T. extra-virgin olive oil
1 T. balsamic vinegar
2 T. orange juice

Arrange 1 cup of salad greens on each of four serving plates. Scatter the kiwi slices, mandarin oranges and red onion over each salad. In a small bowl, whisk together the oil, vinegar and orange juice. Drizzle about 1 tablespoon of the dressing mixture over each salad.

Serving size: *¼ of recipe (1¼ cups salad)*
Calories: *74*
Fat: *3.6 g*

Broccoli
Garden Toss

¾ C. small fresh broccoli flowerets

¾ C. small fresh cauliflower flowerets

1 small sweet red pepper, seeded and chopped

1 T. extra-virgin olive oil

3 T. white wine vinegar

¼ tsp. salt

¼ tsp. pepper

⅛ tsp. garlic powder

Combine the broccoli and cauliflower flowerets in a microwave-safe baking dish; add ¼ cup water. Cover the dish with plastic wrap and microwave on high for 4 to 6 minutes, or until the vegetables are tender but crisp. Drain the vegetables and add the sweet pepper; toss gently. In a jar with a tight-fitting lid, combine the oil, vinegar, salt, pepper and garlic powder. Cover with the lid and shake vigorously until combined. Pour the mixture over the vegetables and toss until evenly coated. Cover and chill for at least 30 minutes before serving.

Serving size: *¼ of recipe (½ cup salad)*
Calories: *45.5*
Fat: *3.5 g*

Spiced
Grape Salad

¼ C. low-fat vanilla yogurt
⅛ tsp. ground cinnamon
⅛ tsp. ground cardamom
1 C. seedless green grapes, halved
1 C. seedless red grapes, halved

In a medium bowl, combine the yogurt, cinnamon and cardamom; mix well. Add the green and red grapes; toss until evenly coated. Cover and chill in the refrigerator until ready to serve.

Serving size: *¼ of recipe (½ cup salad)*
Calories: *70*
Fat: *0.7 g*

Low-Fat
Potato Salad

Makes 6 servings

6 medium potatoes, peeled
6 hard-boiled eggs, yolks removed, whites chopped
2 stalks celery, thinly sliced
½ C. seeded and chopped red or green bell pepper
½ C. chopped onion
1¼ C. fat-free mayonnaise
1 T. white vinegar
½ C. prepared yellow mustard
¼ C. pickle relish
1½ tsp. salt
½ tsp. pepper

Place the potatoes in a large pot; fill with water to cover potatoes by 1". Place the pot over medium-high heat and boil the potatoes for 20 minutes. Drain the potatoes and set aside to cool. Chill the potatoes in the refrigerator until ready to prepare. Just before serving, cut the potatoes into cubes. In a large bowl, combine the chopped egg whites, celery, bell pepper, onion, mayonnaise, vinegar, mustard, relish, salt and pepper; mix well. Add the potatoes and toss until evenly coated and mixed. Serve immediately or chill in the refrigerator until ready to serve.

Serving size: ⅙ *of recipe (about 1 cup salad)*
Calories: 206
Fat: 2.3 g

Stuffed Zucchini Boats

Makes 4 servings

2 medium zucchinis, halved lengthwise
½ T. extra-virgin olive oil
1 small onion, chopped
1 clove garlic, crushed
2 oz. button mushrooms, sliced
½ tsp. ground coriander
¾ tsp. ground cumin
½ (15.5 oz.) can chick peas, rinsed and drained
1 T. lemon juice
2 T. chopped fresh parsley
Sea salt and pepper to taste

Preheat the oven to 350°. Spray a 1-quart baking dish with non-stick cooking spray; set aside. Scoop the flesh out of the zucchini halves to make four canoe-like shells. Chop the removed zucchini flesh and set aside. Set the shells in the prepared baking dish. Heat the oil in a large skillet over medium heat. Add the onion; sauté for 5 minutes. Stir in the garlic; sauté for 2 minutes. Stir in the chopped zucchini and mushrooms; sauté for an additional 5 minutes. Stir in the coriander, cumin, chick peas, lemon juice, parsley, salt and pepper; mix until well combined. Divide the mixture into four portions. Stuff each zucchini shell with one of the portions. Bake for 30 to 40 minutes, or until the zucchini shells are tender.

Serving size: *1 stuffed zucchini half*
Calories: *107*
Fat: *2.7 g*

Quinoa with Black Beans

1 tsp. vegetable oil

1 onion, chopped

3 cloves garlic, minced

¾ C. uncooked quinoa

1½ C. low-sodium vegetable broth

1 tsp. ground cumin

¼ tsp. cayenne pepper

Salt and pepper to taste

1 C. fresh or frozen corn kernels

2 (15 oz.) cans black beans, rinsed and drained

½ C. chopped fresh cilantro

Heat the oil in a medium saucepan over medium heat. Add the onion and garlic; sauté until lightly browned. Mix the quinoa into the saucepan and add the vegetable broth; season with cumin, cayenne pepper, salt and pepper. Bring the mixture to a boil, cover and reduce the heat to medium-low; simmer for 20 minutes. Stir the corn into the saucepan and continue to simmer for about 5 minutes, or until heated through. Fold in the black beans and cilantro.

Serving size: ⅒ *of recipe (about ¾ cup)*
Calories: 154
Fat: 1.7 g

Rosemary
Roasted Potatoes

2 lbs. red potatoes, cut into quarters

2 T. vegetable oil

1 tsp. salt

½ tsp. pepper

½ tsp. dried rosemary

Preheat the oven to 450°. Place the potatoes on a rimmed baking sheet. Drizzle the oil over the potatoes and sprinkle with the salt, pepper and rosemary; toss until evenly coated. Spread out the potatoes in a single layer. Bake for 20 minutes, stirring every 5 minutes. Serve immediately.

Serving size: *¼ of recipe (1½ to 2 cups potatoes)*
Calories: *227*
Fat: *7.3 g*

Mashed Turnip & Potatoes

Makes 6 servings

1 large turnip, peeled and cubed
3 white potatoes, peeled and cubed
¼ C. skim milk
1 tsp. sugar
3 T. unsalted butter, divided
¾ tsp. salt
¼ tsp. pepper

Preheat the oven to 375°. Place the turnip and potatoes in a large pot; fill with water to cover turnip and potatoes by 1". Place the pot over medium-high heat and boil for 25 to 30 minutes. Drain the turnip and potatoes; set aside to cool. Mix the milk, sugar and 2 tablespoons butter into the turnip and potatoes. Season with salt and pepper; mash until slightly lumpy. Transfer the mashed mixture to a small baking dish; dot with remaining butter. Cover the baking dish loosely and bake for 15 minutes. Remove the cover and continue baking for about 8 minutes, or until lightly browned.

Serving size: *⅙ of recipe (about ¾ cup mashed potatoes)*
Calories: *100*
Fat: *6 g*

Tasty Breaded Brussels

Makes 6 servings

¾ lb. fresh Brussels sprouts
½ tsp. salt
2 T. butter, melted, divided
2 T. grated Parmesan cheese
2 T. dried bread crumbs
⅛ tsp. garlic powder
⅛ tsp. pepper
⅛ tsp. seasoning salt

Wash and trim any broken leaves from the Brussels sprouts. Cut an ⅛" deep "x" in the stem end of each Brussels sprout. Place the Brussels in a medium pot and cover with water. Stir in the salt and place over medium-high heat; bring to a boil. Reduce the heat, cover and simmer for about 6 minutes, or until the Brussels are tender; drain. Preheat the oven broiler to high heat. Transfer the Brussels to a 1-quart baking dish; sprinkle with 1 tablespoon melted butter and toss until evenly coated. In a small bowl, combine the remaining 1 tablespoon butter, Parmesan cheese, bread crumbs, garlic powder, pepper and seasoning salt; sprinkle over the Brussels and toss lightly. Place under the broiler for about 5 minutes or until the crumb mixture is lightly browned. Serve immediately.

Serving size: *⅙ of recipe (about 6 Brussels sprouts)*
Calories: *75*
Fat: *4.6 g*

Guilt-Free
Zesty Coleslaw

Makes 8 servings

8 C. coarsely shredded cabbage
1 large carrot, grated
½ C. fat-free mayonnaise
2 T. white wine vinegar
2 T. pineapple juice
3 T. spicy brown mustard
1½ T. sugar
⅛ tsp. pepper

In a large bowl, combine the cabbage and carrot; toss until mixed. In a small bowl, whisk together the mayonnaise, vinegar, pineapple juice, mustard, sugar and pepper. Pour the dressing over the cabbage; toss until evenly coated and well mixed. Cover the bowl and chill in the refrigerator until ready to serve.

Serving size: ⅛ *of recipe (about 1 cup coleslaw)*
Calories: 45
Fat: 0.5 g

Scalloped Corn & Broccoli

1 (15 oz.) can creamed corn

2 eggs, beaten

2 T. sugar

2 T. flour

1 tsp. salt

½ C. shredded Cheddar cheese

1 (10 oz.) pkg. frozen chopped broccoli, thawed and drained

Preheat the oven to 350°. In a large bowl, combine the creamed corn, eggs, sugar, flour and salt; stir until well combined. Fold in the cheese and broccoli; mix well. Transfer the mixture to a 1½-quart baking dish. Bake for 1 hour.

Serving size: *⅙ of recipe (about ½ cup)*
Calories: *162*
Fat: *3.75 g*

Seasoned Green Beans & Cherry Tomatoes

Makes 6 servings

1½ lbs. green beans, trimmed and cut into 2" pieces
¼ C. butter
1 T. sugar
¾ tsp. garlic salt
¼ tsp. pepper
1½ tsp. chopped fresh basil
2 C. halved cherry tomatoes

Place the beans in a large saucepan and cover with water; bring to a boil over medium-high heat. Reduce the heat to low and simmer until tender, about 10 minutes. Drain the beans and set aside. Melt the butter in a small saucepan over low heat; stir in the sugar, garlic salt, pepper and basil. Add the tomatoes to the saucepan and cook until softened. Pour the tomato mixture over the green beans and toss gently until well mixed.

Serving size: *⅙ of recipe (about 1 cup)*
Calories: *122*
Fat: *8 g*

Quick Garlic Asparagus

Makes 4 servings

3 T. butter
1 large bunch fresh asparagus
3 cloves garlic, minced

Melt the butter in a large skillet over medium-high heat. Add the asparagus and garlic; cook and stir for about 10 minutes, or until the asparagus is tender.

Serving size: *⅙ of recipe (about 5 asparagus spears)*
Calories: *106*
Fat: *8.9 g*

Dilled Carrots

Makes 6 servings

1 (8 oz.) bag baby carrots
2 T. butter
1 tsp. sugar
½ tsp. salt
½ tsp. dried dillweed

In a large saucepan over medium-high heat, combine the carrots, ½ cup water, butter, sugar, salt and dillweed. Bring the liquid to a boil, reduce the heat to medium-low, cover and simmer for 25 to 30 minutes, or until most of the liquid is absorbed, stirring occasionally.

> **Serving size:** *⅙ of recipe (about 6 baby carrots)*
> **Calories:** *72*
> **Fat:** *4 g*

Feel the Burn!

Lend a helping hand! You'll burn a quick 100 calories by helping a farmer friend bail hay for 9 minutes.

White Wine Herbed Mushrooms

Makes 6 servings

1 T. extra-virgin olive oil
1½ lbs. small white or button mushrooms
1 tsp. Italian seasoning
¼ C. dry white wine
2 cloves garlic, minced
Salt and pepper to taste
2 T. chopped fresh chives

Heat the oil in a large skillet over medium heat. Add the mushrooms to the skillet and sprinkle with Italian seasoning; sauté for 10 minutes. Stir in the white wine and garlic; continue to sauté until most of the wine has been evaporated. Season with salt and pepper; sprinkle with chives. Continue to heat for 1 minute; serve immediately.

Serving size: *⅙ of recipe (about ½ cup mushrooms)*
Calories: *55*
Fat: *2.7 g*

Black Beans & Rice

Makes 10 servings

1 tsp. extra-virgin olive oil
1 onion, chopped
2 cloves garlic, minced
¾ C. uncooked white rice
1½ C. low-sodium vegetable broth
1 tsp. ground cumin
¼ tsp. cayenne pepper
3½ C. canned black beans, rinsed and drained

Heat the oil in a large pot over medium-high heat. Stir in the onion and garlic; sauté for 4 minutes. Stir in the rice and sauté for 2 more minutes. Add the vegetable broth and bring to a boil; cover, reduce the heat to medium-low and simmer for 20 minutes. Remove the pot from the heat and stir in the cumin, pepper and black beans; toss until well mixed.

Serving size: *⅒ of recipe (½ to ¾ cup)*
Calories: *135*
Fat: *0.9 g*

Spiced Brown Rice with Corn

1 C. brown rice
1 T. extra-virgin olive oil
½ tsp. salt
1 C. fresh or frozen corn kernels
½ tsp. dried cilantro
½ tsp. dried cumin

Mix the rice with 2 cups water in a medium saucepan over medium-high heat. Stir in the oil and salt; bring to a boil. Mix in the corn, cilantro and cumin. Reduce the heat to medium-low, cover and let simmer for 45 to 60 minutes, or until most of the liquid has been absorbed.

Serving size: *⅙ of recipe (about ½ cup)*
Calories: *133*
Fat: *3.2 g*

Cheesy & Easy
Twice-Baked Potatoes

Makes 4 servings

2 Idaho potatoes
¼ C. fat-free sour cream
¼ C. crumbled blue cheese
1 tsp. chopped fresh parsley

Preheat the oven to 400°. Pierce the potatoes with a fork and place on the middle baking rack in the oven; bake until tender, about 45 to 50 minutes. Remove the potatoes from the oven and let stand until cool enough to handle. Cut the potatoes in half lengthwise and scoop out the flesh, leaving about ¼" thick shells. In a medium bowl, combine the potato flesh, sour cream, blue cheese and parsley; mash until blended and smooth. Spoon the filling back into the potato shells. Place on a baking sheet and bake for 15 minutes.

Serving size: 1 stuffed potato half
Calories: 169
Fat: 4.1 g

Whole-Wheat Dinner Rolls

½ C. low-fat plain yogurt
¼ C. skim milk
2 T. honey
¼ C. margarine
2 C. bread flour
1 C. whole-wheat flour
1 tsp. salt
1½ tsp. active dry yeast
¼ C. egg substitute

In a small microwave-safe bowl, combine the yogurt, milk, honey and margarine; microwave for 1 minute and stir until the butter is melted. In the container of a bread machine, combine the bread flour, whole-wheat flour, salt and yeast, forming a well in the center. Pour the melted butter mixture and egg substitute into the well. Set the bread machine to the dough cycle. When the cycle is finished, shape the dough into 18 equally-sized rolls. Preheat the oven to 350°. Place the rolls in lightly greased muffin pans, cover with a damp towel and set on top of the preheating oven; let rise for about 30 minutes. Bake for 15 to 20 minutes or until golden brown. Serve warm.

Serving size: *1 roll*
Calories: *132*
Fat: *2.9 g*

Corn Bread Custard

Makes 10 servings

4 C. skim milk

1¼ C. yellow cornmeal

1½ tsp. salt

1 C. fresh or frozen whole kernel corn

⅓ C. chopped green onions

¼ C. unsalted butter, cubed

3 eggs

Preheat the oven to 375°. Spray an 8" square baking dish with non-stick cooking spray. In a medium saucepan over medium heat, whisk together the milk, cornmeal and salt; bring to a boil, whisking until the mixture begins to thicken, about 4 minutes. Reduce the heat to low and continue to cook until thickened, about 20 minutes. Transfer the mixture to a large bowl; stir in the corn, green onions and butter. Separate the eggs. Add the egg yolks to the corn mixture, one at a time, stirring well after each addition. Whip the egg whites until stiff peaks form. Fold the egg whites into the corn mixture. Spread the batter in the prepared pan; bake until puffed and golden brown, about 30 minutes; serve immediately.

Serving size: ¹⁄₁₀ *of recipe (about ½ cup)*
Calories: *168*
Fat: *6.9 g*

INDEX

INDEX

INDEX

Seafood

Soup & Other Stuff

INDEX

Pick-A-Side Dish